The Proverbs Of John Heywood

THE PROVERBS OF JOHN HEYWOOD.

"Then doth he licke his lippes and stroke his beard,
That's glewed together with his slavering droppes
Of yestie ale, and when he scarce can trim
His goutie fingers thus hee'l fillip it,
And with a rotten hem, say 'hey, my hearts !'
Merrie go sorrie ! cocke and pye, my heart !'
But then their saving pennie proverbe comes."

Two Angry Women of Abington, 1599.

THE PROVERBS OF JOHN HEYWOOD.

BEING THE "PROVERBES" OF THAT
AUTHOR PRINTED 1546.

EDITED, WITH NOTES AND INTRODUCTION,

BY JULIAN SHARMAN.

LONDON:

GEORGE BELL AND SONS, YORK STREET,

COVENT GARDEN.

1874.

CHISWICK PRESS :—PRINTED BY WHITTINGHAM AND WILKINS,
TOOKS COURT, CHANCERY LANE.

TO MY FRIEND,

BOURCHIER F. HAWKSLEY, Esq.,

THIS VOLUME IS

DEDICATED.

INTRODUCTION.

HE traditions of old Saxon literature had never been obliterated by rust or utterly defaced by invasion; even after the toll of the curfew, there yet lingered round the Saxon embers the homely folk-speech of Jutes and Angles. But the hidden graces of that English tongue no English Aristotle had attempted to uncover. No earlier Erasmus had arisen to restore the gems of speech and learning; no English Quintilian to knit the scattered threads of idiom together. Everywhere where the English independence was subjected, was the English language as effectually despised.

Yet the Norman in proscribing the ancient literature could hardly hope to extirpate the ancient ways of thought. Still less could he hope to interrupt that flow of tears and laughter, the pathos and the humour which proceed from thought. We know that whatever was memorable or captivating in the old-world literature was accustomed to be recited, until the sense of property in such compositions becoming gradually lost, that grew to be the wit of many which had formerly been the wisdom of one. Such perpetual assumption of authorship would have been in itself sufficient to protect that verbal literature from desuetude, even had not the professional *farceur* worked mightily towards its preservation. The shrewd maxims of their Saxon forefathers had indeed been given over to the use of the meanest of the people's literary caterers, and as the common stock of glee-men and ale-poets, still continued to mingle with mirth and revel as they had done since the days of the Heptarchy. But in the popular adherence to the old charms of speech, we think we perceive a restless importunity to bestow, as it were, upon a fitting recipient that priceless heirloom venerable by reverence and by antiquity. Antiquity was dead, but not without issue. Already patient monastics had begun to embalm the decaying Saxon saws

and sentences in hideous cerements of rhyming Latin;
and to the antiquary who to-day unravels the leonine
verses they have wrought for us, will stand revealed
the sprightly sayings of mediæval England. In this
process we are reminded of nothing so much as the
account given by our first Arctic navigator of the
prodigious thawing of words and consonants that had
long remained congealed in the atmosphere during
the winter nights. In the wintry night of the Norman
conquest, the direction of the English mind was one
long effort to perpetuate and to transmit the pith
and saltness of its bygone literature. An arm is
stretched out, as it were, across three centuries—the
heirloom so often proffered is as often refused—
until the chattel at last is seized, and that by the
hand of Chaucer. It might be idle to assert for an
object so immaterial so definite a claim to antiquity,
but we are not unwilling to believe that the same
vein of wit and cunning which gives vitality to essen-
tially English pages, from a Chaucer to a Dickens, is
part and parcel of the very mine of wisdom whose
produce the followers of Hengist bore away from
Old Saxony.

But the soil wherein the Saxon stem was planted
may still perhaps be bearing herbage of a widely different undergrowth. The doctrines of the Druids,

preserved only by verbal narration, did not altogether perish at the destruction of the Druidic priesthood. In the maxims of Old Gaul and in the cherished sayings of Wales and Cornwall, some little of that traditional wisdom remains. The proverbial triads of the Cymri still perpetuate some facts of history. That the settlers from the " Summer Land,"—from the Tauric Chersonese,—descended here upon these islands is recorded in the Druidic triads. That they recoiled before the invasions of Romans and of Irishmen is there also deplored ; and together with these historical relics are mingled an abundant crop of Druidic maxims, the condensation of ancient British thought.

Another, and undeniably the merriest contributor, has contributed to the proverbial store-house. Two centuries previously, we read that a Duke of Normandy had sent a son to Bayeux to learn Danish ; under the earlier Plantagenets, the young Norman aristocracy might have visited England to learn French. The humbler Englishman may have possessed little aptitude for acquiring the Norman speech, but even the Gurths and Wambas of the time could not fail to be attracted by the light and sparkle which glittered on the surface of the smoother tongue. If the Norman was the best sayer of fine things ; the Englishman was incomparably the best hearer of them. When the smack of novelty had once passed away, those crumbs of merriment which the Frenchman discarded were by the other gratefully retained. In truth the palate of the Norman was gratified only by the crispness and the unexpectedness of the saying. It was the Englishman alone who was capable of luxuriating in its perfect infinity of application. But what wonderful resources were displayed by the Norman mind! The Saxon could look only to his glebe or his farmyard for a simile. The Frenchman had the run of the tavern, the boothie, and the play-house; he brought away dainty morsels from the convent-cell; he imported curious scholar-talk from Paris and Montpellier.

Such, then, being the genealogy of our hereditary folk-lore, it will seem strange that the patrimony should at any time be liable to diminish. Nevertheless it would appear to be the fact that for upwards of a hundred years the people's wisdom was rigidly expugned from whatever prints and writings were intended for preservation. The prejudice of Lord Chesterfield that a national proverb was not becoming to the conversation of a man of breeding, would seem to have held good as well for the fifteenth as for the eighteenth century. It was not until the second de-

cade of the next century that our vernacular literature again began to raise its head.   In what measure
the publication of Heywood's book contributed to
the general restoration it is quite impossible to conjecture, but it is not unreasonable to believe that its
conservative influence was considerable.   But here we
may make room for a fine retrospect as it has been
left us by two of the leading scholars of their day,
Sir Thomas More and Roger Ascham.

" In our forefather's tyme," says Ascham, " when
Papistrie as a standyng poole, covered and overflowed
all England, fewe bookes were read in our tong,
savyng certaine bookes of Chevalrie, as they said, for
pastime and pleasure, which, as some say, were made
in monasteries by idle monkes or wanton chanons, as
one for example, Morte Arthure: the whole pleasure
of which booke standeth in two special poyntes ; in
open maunslaughter and bold bawdrye.   In which
booke, those be counted the noblest knightes that do
kill most men without any quarrell and commit
fowlest advoulteres by subtlest shiftes ; as Sir Launcelote, with the wife of King Arthure, his master ; Syr
Tristram, with the wife of Kynge Marke, his uncle ;
Syr Lamerocke with the wife of King Lote, that was
his owne aunte . . . I know when God's Bible was
banished the court, and Morte Arthure received into
the Prince's chamber."

Prior to him Sir Thomas More writes :—" There is an use nowe a daies worse than amonge the Pagans, that bookes written in our mother's tonges, that be made but for idel men and women to reade, have none other matter but of war and love. . . . What a custome is thys, that a song shall not be regarded, but it bee full of fylthynes, and this the lawes oughte to take hede of, and of those ungracious fokes, such as bee in my countrey in Spayne : Amadise, Florisande, Tirante, Tristane, and Celestina the baude, mother of naughtynes. In Fraunce : Launcelote du Lake, Paris and Vienna, Ponthus and Sidonia, and Melneyne. In Flanders : Flory and Whyte flowre : Leonell and Canomoure, Curias and Florete, Pyramus and Thisbe. In England : Parthenope, Genarides, Hippomadron, Willyam and Meliour, Livius and Arthur, Guye and Bevis, and many other, and some translated out of Latyne into vulgare speaches, as the unsavery conceites of Pogius, and of Aneas Silvius, Gurialus and Lucretia."

Those monastic writings, which, as Ascham had heard, were the work of "wanton canons" or worthless monks, had been too foreign in their antecedents to adhere to the idiom and racy phraseology of foregoing times. The volumes which proceeded from the presses of the early printers were frequently the

most inhistoric of histories or the most wearisome
of romances. But already in Germany and in our
own country, Polydore Vergil and Erasmus had
begun to garner up the treasured sayings of classical
antiquity; and the laureate Skelton, himself a sage
and a classic, had preferred to sound a note better
attuned to the public ear and more pleasing to the
popular imagination. The author of *Elinour Rum-
myng* had taken up the lyre of Chaucer, not indeed as
Chaucer, but as Lydgate had dropped it. Then came
John Heywood. A protegé of Sir Thomas More,
and a familiar intimate of Skelton, Heywood might
well impart to the chancellor, at his house at Chelsea,
selections from the fund of grotesque ribaldry which
he had previously heard, say, at the notorious Three
Cranes. Skelton had set the fashion for coarse
rhymes; Heywood made coarse rhymes fashionable.
There is little doubt that, after the appearance of
Heywood's book in 1546, a new idea or influence was
set working in English literature. It was not, indeed,
that the work possessed intrinsic merit, or that its
appearance was attended with circumstances of public
interest. Rather was it that the author was by means
of this work reminding the public of a property
which the owners were inadvertently losing. That
same meaning which the romancers before him had

attempted to explain with an allegory, Heywood could promptly convey in a proverb. The romancers were rejected; Heywood's volume was hailed with acclaim. It became the most popular of all popular books. Ten times it was sent to press during the sixteenth century. Immediately on its appearance it gave a fillip to the nation's appetite for literary enjoyment; poets, play-writers, and statesmen made capital of its mine of proverbs. The Elizabethan dramatists are brimming with them. One orator delivered a speech in the House of Commons in which a proverb formed the substance of every sentence. Proverbs were adopted everywhere as devices for tapestry, as mottoes for knives, as inscriptions for rings and keep-sakes. Shakespeare speaks of a moderate poetaster as one

> —— whose poesy was
> For all the world like cutler's poetry
> Upon a knife, *Love me and leave me not.*

It cannot be pretended that the volume before us has other claims to respect besides the extraneous one of its being the first assemblage of our colloquial sayings. The due transmission of proverbs, and even catch-words, unmutilated from age to age, has excited so much enquiry of late in the pages of our periodicals, that the editor believes that this attempt at restoring an ancient literary landmark will meet with approbation from other gleaners in the same field of antiquarianism. He also believes, with respect to the accompanying glosses, that so considerable a collection of proverbial antiques has not hitherto been brought together. His reason for setting aside the accumulations of trite sayings in classical or oriental literature is that our own in early English possess a relationship far less equivocal. Little could be gained by illustrating English idiom from the *mots dorés* of a Solon or a Pythagoras; less, by illustrating it from a Zoroaster or a Confucius. Though it may be gratifying to discover that the simile of "no stone unturned" proceeds from a reply of the Delphic oracle, or that the homely figure of "a pinching shoe" takes rise from a passage in the Lives of Plutarch, yet it can be no less interesting to learn that Saint Jerome forebore to look a gift-horse in the mouth, or that the proverbial distich chanted by the insurgents in Wat Tyler's rebellion is found in a Teutonic dress in the German proverbs of Agricola.

To any reader of the dramatists, who is at the same time acquainted with Heywood's collection, a curious incident of authorship will be apparent. Such, at least, we take to be that similarity between certain passages in Heywood's book and passages in the

writings of the more prominent authors of a later
day. Both Heywood's work and the extent of its
popularity were well known to Shakespeare, but it is
not seen that the great master availed himself of the
literary leanings of his audience in order to secure
the applause which almost invariably follows on the
recognition of the adopted sentences of a popular
author. Not so Ben Jonson. In the play of *Eastward Hoe*, which that author composed in conjunc-
tion with Marston and Chapman, the dramatist seems
purposely to have opened a page of Heywood that
he might point the dialogue of his smartest characters. The same tacit understanding existing between
audience and actors as would seem to exist at the
present day, we can imagine the hum of approbation
which followed the delivery of each well-worn saying.
A quotation from one of the more farcical parts of
Eastward Hoe is almost parallel to Heywood's
Proverbs :—

Touchstone. I heare your knight errant is traveld on strange
adventures. Surely, in my mind, your ladiship hath *"fisht faire,
and caught a frogge,"* as the saying is.

     *   *   *   ı *   *   *

Girtrude. Come away, I say, *"hunger drops out at his nose."*
Goulding. O, madam, *"Faire words never hurt the tongue."*
Girtrude. How say you that? You come out with your golde
ends now !

Mistress T. Stay, lady, daughter; good husband!

Touchstone. Wife, *no man loves his fetters, be they made of gold.* I list not ha' my head fastned under my child's girdle; *as shee has brew'd, so let her drinke,* a God's name. She went witlesse to wedding, now she may goe wisely a begging. It is but hony-moone yet with her ladiship: she has coach horses, apparel, jewels yet left: she needs care for no friends, nor take knowledge of father, mother, brother, sister, or any body. When those are pawn'd or spent, perhaps we shall returne into the liste of her acquaintance.

Girtrude. I scorne it, i' faith. Come, Sinne. [*Exit Girtrude.*

Mistress T. O, madam, why doe you provoke your father thus?

Touchstone. Nay, nay, eene *let pride go afore: shame wil follow after,* I warrant you. Come, why doest thou weepe now? Thou art *not the first good cow hast had an il calfe,* I trust.

The same observation would apply to portions of Henry Porter's best-known comedy, *The Two Angry Women of Abington,* which, obscure as it yet is, is mentioned by Charles Lamb as being no whit inferior to the earliest performances of Shakespeare. It is full of business, humour, and merry malice.

It is now time to pass from the consideration of the indirect influence of Heywood's work, to detail some particulars of his career, and notably in his capacity of dramatic author.

" Was not Heywood a satirist?" asks one of the

characters in Mr. Payne Collier's skilful work, *The Poetical Decameron.*

" I presume you mean the elder—John Heywood," rejoins another.

" I mean that Heywood who is the author of one of the most witty and entertaining pieces in Dodsley's Collection."

Turning to the theatrical repository here mentioned, we discover that the performance which has so deservedly procured Mr. Collier's eulogy is the one bearing the eccentric title of *Four P's.* The further title—one is involuntarily reminded by it of the traditional three R's—proceeds to explain that the piece is a facetious dialogue held between a Pardoner, a Palmer, a Pothicary, and a Pedler. It is worthy of note that though written by one of the most rigid and bigoted of Catholics and at a time when the tumult of opinions was at its height, the satire of this play is especially directed against the abuses of the Romish communion. As a Catholic of the sixteenth century Heywood went further than a Protestant of the next, in exposing and bringing to just ridicule the enemies alike of the old faith and the new. The religious charlatan who could open the gates of heaven with the rich man's purse-strings; the sanctimonious quack who purchased ease and affluence by a systematic trifling with the souls of his community; these and other types of the monastic character, unhappily but too abundant in his day, found little mercy from the unscrupulous yet unvindictive satire of Heywood.

A speech of the Palmer opens the comedy:—

> At Hierusalem have I bene,
>   Before Chryste's blessed sepulture;
> The mount of Calvary have I sene,
>   A holy place ye may be sure.
>
> *　*　*　*　*
>
> Then at Rhodes also I was,
> And round about to Amias,
> At Saynt Toncomber and Saynt Tronion,
> At Saynt Botolph and Saynt Anne of Buckston.
> On the hylles of Armeny, where I saw Noe's arke,
> With holy Job and Saynt George in Southwarke,
> And at the good rood of Dagnam.

He is interrupted by the Pardoner assuring him that such remote pilgrimages are altogether unnecessary for securing salvation. He might have obtained pardon and stayed at home.

> Geve me but a peny or two pens,
> And as sone as the soule departeth hens,
> In halfe an houre, or three quarters at the moste,
> The soule is in heaven with the Holy Ghost.

The Poticary and the Pedler then join the company; each begins to assert for himself a superior claim to the gratitude of his fellows. " Whose agency is more potent in love?" urges the Pedler. " That is of first importance in the affairs of this world," so admits the Poticary, "but who is it but myself who hastens so many people to the next?" At last tired of disputing their pre-eminence, it is agreed that the disputants shall compete for the mastery by telling fibs ; the greatest liar to be thenceforth recognized as chief and primus of this exemplary four. The task, says the Pedler, cannot be a heavy one, as they are all accustomed to it ; while he, possessing no little skill in the art of lying, is constituted umpire. It having been decided to make the trial in succession, the Pardoner takes the lead by relating the virtues of his relics. His inventions concerning the jaw-bone of All Hallows and the slippers of the Seven Sleepers are acknowledged as belonging merely to the class of respectable mediocrity. But no sooner is the Poticary called on for his lie, than he declares the Palmer to be an honest man. This was indeed a falsehood of the first magnitude, but it is confessed by the umpire that he is still unable to determine the quantity of credit exactly due to each. To meet the difficulty it is proposed that each shall recount some marvellous adventure, not apocryphal at all, but falling within the strict letter of fact.

The Poticary who leads off with a story of a wonderful cure is soon distanced by the recital of the Pardoner. This worthy seriously details the circumstances of a visit to hell which he had undertaken to regain the soul of a lamented lady intimate :—

> A frende of myne, and lykewyse I
> To her agayne was as frendly.

He had first, he said, enquired at the gates of purgatory whether a person answering to the description which he gave of her had recently been admitted ; but when informed to the contrary :—

> Alas ! thought I, she is in hell ;
> For with her lyfe I was so acqueynted
> That sure I thought she was not saynted.

He had accordingly hastened to that locality, where recognizing an old acquaintance in the porter at the gate, he procures a free passport to traverse the satanic realm. Walking arm-in-arm with his old associate, the Pardoner approaches a spot where the denizens of hell are celebrating an infernal orgy. There he is cordially received by the genius of the place, Lucifer himself, and the Pardoner presently advances his suit. He will do the devil a good turn on earth, so he bargains, if in consideration for these promised services, his Majesty will release a certain

soul from his dominions.   When told that it is a
female soul, nothing can exceed the delight of Lucifer.
No subjects, he declares, occasion more disquiet to
the reign of Satan than the women souls whom weary
earth consigns him.   He requests, even implores, that
the Pardoner will send none other of that sex to dis-
turb his subjects' harmony, a wish that the other
readily promises to respect.   Accordingly the woman
is made over to her deliverer, who escorts her to
Newmarket Heath, and there leaves her to her own
devices.

It had appeared to the Pardoner that this piece of
mendacity was far too brazen for the remaining
competitors to surpass, when the Palmer, commenting
on the other's recital, lets fall the stupid observation
that in a long lifetime he had never seen a woman
out of patience.   In later times it would be regarded
as singularly the reverse of a fitting climax that a
drama so skilfully constructed should terminate with
so feeble a situation ; but, in the days of John Heywood, stage exigencies were abundantly satisfied by
such a finale as we see contrived by the irony of the
blundering Palmer.

The interlude of Heywood's which contains in-
ternal proof of having been first written is the *Mery
Playe betwene the Pardoner and the Frere, the Curate*

and neybour Pratte. The fact of Leo X. being mentioned in it as then living fixes the date of its production prior to 1521. Like the interlude we have just noticed, it is conceived in a tone of deep hostility to the established clergy. Like that again its intention is to expose the mischievous impostures of the mendicant orders. A friar and a professional pardon-monger have taken possession of a church, the one to exhort the congregation to benevolence, the other to find purchasers for his saintly relics. The friar is already enlarging on the poverty of his order when the pardoner interrupts the harangue by proclaiming the pretended virtues of his receipts and nostrums.[1] The great toe of the Trinity and the articles of wearing apparel once belonging to the Virgin are amongst the most startling of the Pardoner's relics, a complete catalogue of which is interrupted by the obstinate determination of the mendicant to obtain a hearing. The friar taunts his adversary with the publication of "a ragman's roll of lies," as he emphatically expresses it. The mendicant replies with blows, and the two are coming to close combat

---

[1] Mr. F. J. Furnivall writing in *Notes and Queries*, (4th S. IX. 177) draws attention to the fact that Heywood has incorporated into the Pardoner's speech lines 49-100 of CHAUCER'S *Pardoner's Prologue.*

when the curate, who has been informed of the dis-
turbance, rushes into church thinking to lay violent
hands on the monastic. " Let me alone with this
gentleman," cries his reverence, at the same time
enjoining Master Pratte, who at this juncture appears
on the scene, to deal severely with the layman.   It
is disappointing to find in the conclusion that the
two charlatans, better accustomed to the practice of
pugilism, fare best in the encounter and are suffered
to march off on their several ways.

Two pieces we have next to notice would purport,
from their structural simplicity, to be a product of an
almost aboriginal period of the drama.   In neither is
there promise of an acted story, nor as they proceed
is there any indication of plot or circumstance.   Alike
devoid of " business," the simplest stage appliances
are the only requisites for their production.   Considered as spectacles, the *Play of the Wether* and
the *Play of Love* seem equally unlikely to afford
attraction, but when we consider that these popular
performances amounted to nothing but argumentative
and interminable conversations, we must suppose
such audiences as they did actually command to
have had a keener appreciation for logical subtilty
than any that have since been collected within the
walls of a play-house.

The Play of the Wether gives us a curious table of *dramatis personæ*, which, as it is not a lengthy one, may be here set out.

> Jupiter, a god.
> Merry Reporte, the vyce.
> The gentylman.
> The marchaunt.
> The ranger.
> The water myller.
> The wynde myller.
> The gentylwoman.
> The launder.
> A boy the lest that can play.

The scene opens by Jupiter appearing and proceeding, after the manner of a chorus, to explain the argument of the drama. So great vexation, he declares, had been occasioned to mortals through the perverse disposition of the elements that he had summoned the rulers of the firmament to his judgment seat to answer the charges that had previously been preferred against them. Having appeared at the time appointed, each had complained that his individual endeavours to promote the happiness of man were constantly thwarted by the action of his companions in the celestial government. Saturn had charged Phœbus with melting the morning frost and rendering the labour of the night useless. Phœbus had exclaimed against Phœbe, whose

showers, he complained, were alike prejudicial to
the workings both of frost and heat. Instead of re-
senting this imputation, Phœbe made common cause
with the other complainants, and together they fell
foul of Eolus. He, they said,—

> When he is dysposed his blastes to blow
> Suffereth neyther sone shyne, rayne nor snow.

Jupiter, then, had been invited to arrange the dif-
ferences, and has descended to earth that he might
consider the petitions of such among the mortals
as were aggrieved by the elemental caprices. Merry
Reporte, a certain mercurial intelligence, acts as
medium between Jupiter and the suppliants, and it is
with the spoken commentary of this personage that
the play now concerns itself. The first suitor is a
"gentylman" desiring clear weather without cloud
or mist,

> nor no wynde to blow
> For hurt in hys huntynge.

The merchant prayed for a "mesurable wynde." As
for the ranger, he was so blinded by private interest
as plainly to say—

> there bloweth no wynde at al ;

while the water-miller exclaimed that—

> the wynde was so stout
> The rayne could not fall ;

a statement politely contradicted by the wind-miller,

> Who sayd for the rayne he could no wynde wyn ;
> The water he wysht to be banysht all.

But an applicant of a different complexion was the "goodly dame," who desired neither rain nor sunshine,

> But fayre close wether her beautye to save ;

And the last to appeal were the schoolboy, who wished for nothing better than frost or snowballing, and the poor woman

> that lyveth by laundry,
> Who must have wether hot
> And clere her clothys to dry.

In the end, Jupiter promises to institute such a disposal of the elements that all trades in due season may prosper without injury one to another.

It may here be observed that all the "business" of this comedy is supposed to be transpiring away from the stage, or else to have already taken place. It is in effect nothing but a long recitation, the variety of characters being useful only as supplying the appropriate reliefs in speaking it. At the close, a mutual understanding is come to and all parties are satisfied and depart.

Nearly three hundred years of neglect must have passed over all knowledge of the *Play of Love*, when a unique copy was accidentally discovered by the librarian at the Bodleian Library. Here again are found the same mythical and abstract personages, the same creations who monopolized the drama in its earlier stages, and who were for ever superseded when interlude was displaced by comedy.

A Lover not Beloved and the object of his regard, a Woman Beloved not Loving, discourse upon the relative painfulness of their respective states of feeling. The lady with more charity, and with nearly as little reason as her pursuer, insists that the more pain falls to the lot of those who are the objects of a passion which they cannot reciprocate. The audience may have felt a desire to know more of this philosophic maiden, but could not fail to agree with the Lover not Beloved when he replies—

> I say and will verefy,
> Of all pains the most incomparable pain,
> Is to be a lover not loved again.

The conflict of opinions is now heightened by the appearance of the Lover Loved, an anxious though self-satisfied character, and Neither Loved nor Loving, a personage who bears the burden of the comic portion of the play. The former, having thus avowed complete satisfaction with his condition,—

> —— love is my feader,
> Love is my lord, and love is my leader !

meets with direct contradiction from the perfectly absolute Neither Loved nor Loving, who intimates that the other does not know his own mind, and that his alone is the most peaceful situation. The *dénouement* shows all parties agreeing to regard one another on an equality of happiness and misfortune. The few words spoken to the audience at the end of the drama bespeak a high standard of stage morality in the first years of the sixteenth century:—

> Since such contention may hardly accord
> In such kind of love as here hath been meant,
> Let us seek the Love of that loving Lord,
> Who to suffer passion for love was content.

A Mery Play between Johan Johan, the Husbande; Tyb, his Wyfe; and Syr Jhon, the Preest, is certainly the most farcical and not the least amusing of Heywood's pieces. It is also one of the coarsest; but its coarseness is of a kind that would be found entertaining in no age but the age which produced it, and even then is too imprurient to be morally hurtful or offensive. This meagre play, in spite of its obscenity, or perhaps by reason of its obscenity, yet remains a relic of an order of things that have long passed away, and brings down to us a savour of ideas that have long since perished. The rural clergyman, whose visits were as dreaded at the homestead as a descent by caterans on the granary or poultry yard, had actually a beau-ideal in sixteenth century life. The type of character was so fully recognized, and was held to furnish such excellent staple for buffoonery, that right reverend prelates did not feel it derogatory from their calling to witness a popular *exposé* of the peccadilloes of their own clergy. Of the piece before us it is sufficient to say that the village priest does not fail to answer expectation both in his conversation and behaviour, neither can we perceive him to be the least distinguishable from the hero of the story.

The last of Heywood's pieces, one which yet remains a manuscript in the Harleian Library, is a dialogue between three persons, named respectively John, James, and Jerome. The title which has more lately been bestowed on this performance is *A Dialogue on Wit and Folly;* John arguing the superiority of the life of a wise man, and James maintaining the greater comfort of the witless one. The latter defends the strong position that pain of body is less grievous than that of mind. But, replies John,—

> The student's pain is oft pleasantly mixt
> In feeling what fruit by his study is fixt.

To which James, with an ability which proclaims him in no way allied to the "witless" whose cause he argues, makes reply,—

> The laborers labour quiteth that at a whip
> In feeling the fruit of his workmanship.
> As much delight carters in carts neat trimmed
> As do students in books with gold neat limned.

Adding, with no little feeling,—

> Less is the peril and less is the pain
> The knocking of knuckles which fingers doth strain,
> Than digging in the heart, or drying of the brain.

Before dismissing the plays of John Heywood, it is incumbent on us to notice this author's position with regard to the history of the English stage. He is, unless we greatly err, the originator, nay, the inventor of our native drama. That distinction, once accorded to the author of *Gammer Gurton* in 1560, to the author of *Roister Doister*, to the author of *Misogenus*, may safely be transferred from their unconscious shoulders to those of the author of the *Four P's*, about the year 1530. It is true that stage performances, with play-book and words, with scaffolding and apparatus, had existed long before the time of Heywood. They had existed, as they will always continue to exist, wherever men are obedient to the instinct of personation. They existed in Troy, in Thebes, in Baalbec, if, as we may believe, that in those cities men took delight in identifying themselves with imaginary characters more or less debased

or exalted.   But as yet in England, no play or
comedy, that is, no spoken story, had ever been conceived by dramatist, or entered into the heart of man
to perform.   Selections from the Old and New Testa-
ments ; from the Pentateuch, and from the Apocalypse,
had for generations been represented, and had quite
succeeded in satisfying the popular notion of what
was demanded in a stage play.   But these Biblical
performances must have differed from the product of
the later drama in the same way that a street recitation by an old Greek rhapsodist must have differed
from a performance of the *Electra*.   People in this
country were so satisfied with a mimic representation
of the deluge, or the miracle of the loaves and fishes,
that they overlooked the fact that additional amusement might be gained by closely following the drama
of antiquity.   The models were actually in their possession, and yet the owners did not bethink themselves to copy.   But when we recollect the half-serious
moral that is banteringly conveyed in Charles Lamb's
most charming essay ; when we remember the interval
that elapsed in the progress of printing between the
period of block-books and the obvious advance to
type that was movable, we cannot be surprised at the
gap subsisting between the two ages of the drama, or
wonder at the two thousand years that had almost

elapsed before the *Menæchmi* of Plautus had developed into the *Comedy of Errors.*

The line of demarcation between the two periods of stage history must of necessity be an arbitrary one. We prefer to place it at the point where the Bible disappears from the hustings and secular subjects are for the first time introduced. Following our own rule, we shall have no hesitation in claiming the play of the *Pardoner and the Frere* as our earliest comedy, and distinguishing Heywood as our earliest dramatic author. Though forestalled in this respect in other countries of Europe, Heywood may still be said to have beaten his forerunners on the score of originality. Heywood's plays are Gothic in their extraction; those of his contemporaries on the continent draw vitality from Rome and Athens. In France, so soon as the *Confrérie de la Passion* had found strength to throw off its spiritual encumbrances, the stage was burdened with Medeas and Agamemnons. In Germany as yet no drama had arisen, but in Italy both Trissino and Rucellai drew boldly on the comedies of Terence. Heywood, on the contrary, looked only for his characters to the heroes of the fields and hedge-rows. They accordingly are most usually either tramps, or parsons, or cozeners; but his success depending only upon the plaudits of citizen and apprentice, of Cheapside madam or Wapping "waist-coatier," it is not greatly remarkable that a hearty reception was accorded.

We know not for how long the plays of John Heywood continued to hold the stage, but they must inevitably have fallen into discredit upon the first approach of the Elizabethans. In 1633, exactly a century after the publication of Heywood's plays, we find Ben Jonson, in the last play which he was ever permitted to give to the world, pointing unmerited ridicule at the name of Heywood. The play in which Jonson satirises our author is the *Tale of a Tub*, and the scene is that in which the wise men of Finsbury are arranging the preliminaries of a new piece which they have undertaken to exhibit, with the *Tale of a Tub* as its title. Its author,

> Medlay the joiner,
> The only man at a disguise in Middlesex,

by whom Inigo Jones is intended, considers it necessary to view the tubs and washing appliances the better to stimulate his imagination. The squire accordingly directs them to inspect his washhouse, adding—

> Spare us no cost, either in boards or hoops
> To architect your tub : have you ne'er a cooper
> At London, call'd Vitruvius ? send for him :
> Or old John Heywood, call him to you to help.

In searching for a clue to our author's parentage, we gave preference to the neighbourhood of the court as the place wherein to discover the parents or family connections who would naturally have been the means of procuring him his early employment in the household. Two persons of his name are found mentioned in the State papers, both being under rather than above the middle station, and both being dependents in the royal establishment. One is a William Heywood, yeoman of the guard, whose name is constantly occurring as the receiver of sixpence a day, seemingly some perquisite of a yeoman of the crown. In a curious account, which, among other items, also records a payment to " The Boy Bishop at Westminster," this sixpenny fee appears converted into a permanent pension.

The one other Heywood whose position might be supposed to tally with that of the father of the proverbialist, is a William Heywood, described as " King's joiner" in the entries of the treasury accounts. In 1514, this individual was at work on the "Great Harry;" and six years later, at the pageant of the Field of the Cloth of Gold, he held a place in the retinue of the King. The position, it is true, he shared in company of " yeomen bit-makers" and " sergeant saddlers ;" and the pay of twelve-pence per day which he received while on this expedition, would seem to bespeak him of the class of skilled mechanics. It remains quite conjectural whether either of these persons can be identified as John Heywood's relative ; but we cannot think it improbable that the father of the " singing-man" at court was no other than this William Heywood, engaged, as we find him to have been, in supplying furniture and equipments to the king's buffoons at Greenwich and St. James'.

In the first years of the reign of Henry VIII., four separate companies of comedians were maintained for the royal amusement. Two only were established on a permanent footing ; the two others, namely, the " Gentlemen" and the " Children " of the Chapel, playing occasionally, and receiving respectively £10, and £6 13*s*. 4*d*. for their performances. Attached to this latter company of performers we find John Heywood, who must have been quite a child at the date (1515), when the book of payments first makes mention of him. He then drew eight-pence a day as his salary. Five years later, he is receiving a quarterly income of one hundred shillings, that amount appearing to have been "synger wages," as a manuscript pay-book now in the chapter-house at Westminster has chronicled it. So small however is the stock of knowledge that we actually possess with regard to

John Heywood, that from a passing allusion in a comedy, we are ready to infer that at this period he had already commenced the business of a play-writer; and it is perhaps the same paucity of materials which makes us willing to conclude that he had started as an independent manager, when, a few years subsequently, we find a sensible deduction in the amount of his regular salary.

On comparing the receipts of Heywood with others of a like nature, we discover the sum of £20 per annum to have been the amount of honorarium usually bestowed. Such is the sum paid annually to " Vincent Voulp painter," to " the King's voulteger," and to " Nicholas Craser an estronymer." It is noticeable also that the same sum exceeds by nearly one half the amount annually paid for the services of " Pirro the French cook."

The publication of the *Cheque Book of the Chapel Royal,* so ably edited by Dr. Rimbault, has enabled us to elucidate a previously unexplained point in the career of Heywood. That the plebeian singing-boy of the royal chapel should be found a student at Oxford University, that he should have shared the friendship of More· and the confidence of Queen Mary, and should finally become possessor of estates in several English counties, appear to be circumstances incom-

patible with the known indignity of his profession.
But the *Liber Niger Domini Regis*, a manuscript
cited in Dr. Rimbault's work, admits us to a view of
the economy of this semi-religious establishment, and
supplies information which allows us to account for
the singing-boy's promotion. First, directing the
whole affairs of this priestly corporation, but taking
no part in the liturgical services of the church, was
placed a resident dean. Beneath him, and in order of
seniority, came twenty-four chaplains of the chapel.
It is singular to read of their daily allotments—the
dean's allowance of three loaves, the chaplain's mess
of meat and portion of spice and wine, the latter
however allowable only after an evening service. To
a share in these benefits, the lay portion of the chapelry
were likewise entitled, whose sum total of eleven persons consisted of a " Master of Songe," two Epistellers,
or readers of the Epistles, and eight Children of the
Chapel. At the time, then, that Heywood entered
the chapel choir, a restricted yet honourable career
was presented to a youth of musical proficiency. He
might at least aspire to become an " Episteller," or,
taking holy orders, would in due course arrive at the
full dignity of King's chaplain. But as a soprano
voice was far more highly valued in this establishment than either eloquence or scholarship, an outlet

was found for elderly choristers by draughting them off, at his majesty's expense, to the Universities of Oxford or Cambridge.[1] Of this privilege we must suppose Heywood to have availed himself, as we find him to have been entered as a student at Broadgate, now Pembroke College, Oxford.

It is somewhat remarkable that materials for a biography of John Heywood can but with difficulty be recovered from the published remains of his century. After quitting the University, it is probable that he almost immediately took up the profession of theatrical instructor to a company of performing children, at the same time holding on to his emoluments in the household. But of his career as a public caterer no record has come down to us, indeed, his long connection with the stage is evidenced only by desultory notices in private account books, more particularly those used in the royal household in regulating the daily expenses. In one of these, as early as the

---

[1] And when any of these children comene to be xviij years of age, and their voices change, ne cannot be preferred in this chappelle, the nombere being full, then yf they will assente, the Kyng assynethe them to a College of Oxeford or Cambridge of his foundation, there to be at fynding and studye both suffytyently, tylle the King may otherwise advaunce them.—*MS. Harleian*, (293, 642).

year 1526, mention is made of a quarterly salary of fifty shillings, paid by way of retainer to secure Heywood's services in the King's musical establishment. Again in 1537, a payment to Heywood of two pounds occurs among the items of Princess Mary's expenditure and mention of a like disbursement is also found in the privy purse accounts of Princess Elizabeth. Both sums are in remuneration for the performances of Heywood's children. Of these identical performances no account has been preserved, but a memorial of a similar celebration that has come down to us, is not the least curious of the curiosities connected with the stage. From this document we gather some particulars of the performance of a Latin play, acted at Greenwich before Henry VIII. and visitors from France, Maréchal Montmorency, the Bishop of Rouen and Monsieur d'Humières. The *entrepreneur* on this occasion was not John Heywood, but the Head Master of St. Paul's School, John Rightwise, better known to fame in connection with Lyly's Latin Grammar. The play, which was the work of Rightwise himself, and was performed by his own pupils, aimed at heaping ridicule on Luther and the faith of the reformers. When we say that the characters in this piece bear the names of Ecclesia, Heresy and False-Interpretation, the theological nature of the entertainment will be readily surmised. Such companies of juvenile comedians as that which Heywood conducted were the object of considerable animosity among maturer actors, and Shakespeare himself had afterwards to complain of their counter-attractiveness. Ben Jonson, on the contrary, entrusted his best plays to their performing, and on the death of Salathiel Pavey, one of the children, most admiringly writes,—

> He did play old men so duly,
> That, sooth, the Parcæ thought him one,
> He played so truly.

In the *Metamorphosis of Ajax*, 1596, we observe that Sir John Harrington commiserates Heywood as having so narrowly escaped "the jerke of the six-stringed whip." The circumstance alluded to occurred in 1544, when our author, relying too implicitly perhaps on the protection of his friends at court, was so daring and uncompromising as to deny the spiritual supremacy of the King. The terror of the situation, however, appears to have prevailed, for the unfortunate dramatist was permitted to expiate his offences by appearing at Paul's Cross, and there proclaiming a rigmarole of recantations, to which, as we are aware, the firm inflexibility of his opinions would never have permitted him conscientiously to subscribe. "I come hither at this time, good people!" he begins, "willinglye and of mine own desyrouse suit, to show and declare unto you briefly, first of all, the great and inestimable clemency and mercifulness of my most sovereign and redoubted prince the kings majesty, the which his highness hath most graciously used towards me a wretch, most justly and worthily condemned to die for my manifold and outrageous offences. For whereas," he continues, "his majesty's supremacy hath so often been opened unto me both by writing and speaking (if I had had grace either to open my eyes to see it, or mine ears to hear it), to be surely and certainly grounded and established upon the very true way of God ; yet for lack of grace, I have most wilfully and obstinately suffered myself to fall to such blindness, that I have not only thought that the Bishop of Rome hath been, and ought to be, taken the chief and supreme head of the universal church of Christ in earth ; but also, like no true subject, concealed and favoured such as I have known or thought to be of the same opinion. For the which most detestable treasons and untruths, I here most humbly and with all my heart, first of all axe the king's majesty forgiveness, and secondarily all the world."[1]

---

[1] MS. Lambeth. *Bonner Register*, fol. 61. Fox's *Acts and Monuments*, v. 538.

Without any direct authority for the assertion, Heywood has been numbered among the merry fellows who occupied the position of professed jester at the Court of our English Kings. Such an one, it was currently said, could not be a wise man to take the place and could not be a fool to keep it. It is certain that the clowns and merry-andrews whom the Plantagenet and even the Tudor kings loved to have constantly about them, were frequently men of fair literary attainments and of good social standing. So long ago as the eleventh century, a chartered fool had amassed so considerable a treasure in the exercise of his vocation, that the possessions for long after held at Walworth by the see of Canterbury, came by his bequest to be the property of the cathedral church. Not only the jester of Edmund Ironside, but the *cantatores* and *joculatores* of the sterner Norman princes carried away huge proceeds to enhance the comfort of their private lives. At the court of William I. the jester Berdic is said to have retired with a grant of five carucates of land and the lordship of five towns as his pension ; and the magnificent hospital now existing in Smithfield is reported to have been primarily erected with the gains of the licensed jester of Henry I. Arguing from these precedents, it has been presumed that the presents and pensions repeatedly granted to

John Heywood corroborate the supposition that he also is among the King's jesters. The property Heywood accumulated was considerable. First of all we discover that in 1521, an annuity of ten marks was granted to "John Heywood, the King's servant" chargeable on the rentals of two manors in Northamptonshire formerly enjoyed by a certain Thomas Farthing.[1] Again in 1558, five days before Queen Mary's death, there was granted to him under the description of "John Heywood gentleman" the manor of Bulmer in Yorkshire, lately the property of Sir John Bulmer who had become attainted for his complicity in the Pilgrimage of Grace.[2] When, in 1577, a commission was appointed to enquire into the lands and goods of our author and his wife, they found him to have been possessed for life of certain lands at a nominal rental, of which Heywood also held a reversion. Also that Eliza Heywood had land of £5 yearly value which had passed by grant to their daughter Elizabeth. They also found that he held a lease from the Queen of lands in Kent worth £100, which was forfeited by reason of his political offences. Another authority states that he was pos-

---

[1] *State Papers.* Henry VIII. iii. 1186.
[2] *State Papers.* Domestic. XIV. 8.

sessed of customary lands in Hertfordshire, at North Mimms.

We have noticed Queen Mary's death-bed gift to John Heywood, and it is easy to perceive that this was not the only kind office that the zealous Queen performed for him. Probably Heywood's rescue from execution was due to the royal lady's intervention, as it is certain that between the Princess and the singing-man there had existed a long and honourable intimacy. He is the English Rizzio without the tragedy, also, it may be mentioned, without the scandal.

"What wind blew you to court?" asked the Queen, as one day Heywood made his appearance.

"Two," replied the favourite, "especially the one to see your Majesty."

"We thank you for that," said Queen Mary, "but what is the other?"

"That your Grace," he replied, "may see me."

Another time, as it is recorded in Ben Jonson's *Conversations* with Drummond, he came so rudely into the presence that the Queen herself had to interfere. "She had made him so brave," she said, "that he had almost misknowen himself." When she was at the age of eighteen he had composed a poem in her praise, and though the verses have been adduced as an instance of "his poetic policy," it should be remembered that the piece of flattery was bestowed at a time when the object of it was friendless and in disgrace. At her coronation, Heywood took a leading part in the pageant and festivities, and composed another copy of laudatory verses. Even in her last moments, Heywood was permitted to be present, and then, as we have seen, his service and his friendship were not suffered to pass unrecognised or unrewarded.

We have already spoken of Heywood as a dramatist, it now remains for us to notice him as a poet. His verse has not attained to equal notoriety with his dramas; for among a coterie of bad poets, Heywood is easily distinguished as the worst. He has written little that soars higher than the merest doggerel. Of his epigrams, six hundred in number, not one has found a place in the English anthology. Of his best we will only say that they are as puerile as the worst of Martial's, and nearly as indelicate. His single epic, upon which its author must have staked his poetic reputation, may at one time have found place among the other controversial writings of that century; though probably no one—unless Dr. Doran be an exception—has since had the boldness to peruse it. But the historian of Court Fools, after toiling to the end of the last stanza, is convinced that the "Spider and the Fly" of John Heywood is not nearly so entertaining as is the same poem by the free-and-easy poet, Tom Hudson. Not having studied our author's weightiest production, we can offer no opinion on it; but the Proverbs—which we have read—could scarcely be out-done in the way of dense and stupid poetasting. But still in the face of this conviction we will yet maintain, and in this view we shall not be wanting for supporters, that the store of sayings and adages which the old Court Jester has collected, are worthy of preservation as an antiquity of literature and a land-mark in the history of the English mind.

It now only remains for us to add that the edition we have used in our present version of the Proverbs, is that published in 1598, being the last that issued from the press. We have selected the later impression as being more free from corruptions; though the first edition, that of 1546, is the more valuable as it is but very rarely met with. The unwieldiness of Heywood's own title must be our excuse for suppressing it in this version, and the original having changed its appearance so completely in our hands, will perhaps justify the slight fraud upon our author.

We proceed to give his title exactly as we find it; remarking that the latter portion of the title-page alludes to another and distinct work :—

THE WORKES OF JOHN HEIWOOD NEWLIE IM-PRINTED. NAMELIE A DIALOGUE, WHEREIN ARE PLEASANTLIE CONTRIVED THE NUMBER OF ALL THE EFFECTUALL PROVERBS IN OUR ENGLISH TONGUE: COMPACT IN A MATTER CONCERNING TWO MANER OF MARIAGES. TOGETHER WITH THREE HUNDRED EPIGRAMMES UPON THREE HUN-DRED PROVERBES. ALSO A FOURTH, FIFTH AND SIXTH HUNDREDTH OF OTHER VERY PLEASANT, PITHIE AND INGENIOUS EPIGRAMMES. *London.* 1598.

With respect to the preface the editor begs to state that he has refrained from the usual course of supplying every chance mention of an author's name which may with great pains be discovered in obscure contemporary literature. He has preferred to give only such facts and surmises as may be new to the biographer, or such remarks and reflections as these may give rise to. He has already traced the revival of old saws which followed the publication of Heywood's book. But previous to penning these last

d

lines, he has lighted upon a speech in a coeval comedy which bears him out in the justness of his deductions. The play is the one which is well known as the master-piece of Decker, and the proverb-revival is plainly aimed at when one of the buffo-characters begins to quote learnedly from a cheese-trencher. Quaint applications for sentences and maxims have since become more common; but in this incident in Decker's comedy we are strikingly reminded of that unfortunate poem by Sir Bland Burges, which Lord Byron declares having read on the lining of a trunk at Malta.—"And if you don't believe me," adds the poet, "I will buy a port-manteau to quote from."

JULIAN SHARMAN.

Kensington, *March,* 1874.

PROVERBS OF JOHN HEYWOOD.

THE PREFACE.

MONG other things profiting in our
tong,
Those which much may profit both
old and yong:
Such as on their fruit will feede or take holde,
Are our common plaine pithie Proverbs olde.
Some sense of some of which being bare and rude,
Yet to fine and fruitfull effect they allude,
And their sentences include so large a reach,
That almost in all things good lessons they teach.
This write I not to teach, but to touch; for why?
Men know this as well or better then I.

But this and this rest ; I write for this,
Remembring and considering what the pith is,
That, by remembrance of these, Proverbs may grow.
In this tale, erst talked with a friend, I show
As many of them as we could fitly finde
Falling to purpose, that might fall in minde ;
To th'entent that the Reader readily may
Finde them and minde them, when he will alway.

THE FIRST PART.

CHAPTER I.

F mine acquaintance a certaine young
    man
(Being a resorter to me now and than)
Resorted lately, shewing himselfe to be
Desirous to talke at length alone with me
And as we for this a meete place had won,
With this olde proverbe, this young man begon :
Whoso that knew what would be deare,
Should neede be a marchant but one yeare.
Though it, (quoth he), thing impossible bee,
The full sequele of present things to foresee,
Yet doth this proverbe provoke every man,
Politikely, (as man possibly can),
In things to come after, to cast eye before,
To cast out, or keepe in, things for fore store,

As the provision may seeme most profitable,
And the commoditie most commendable.
Into this consideration I am wrought
By two things, which fortune to hands hath brought.
Two women I know, of which twaine the tone
Is a mayde of flowring age, a goodly one ;
Th' other a widow, who so many yeares beares,
That all her whitenes lyeth in her white heares.
This mayde hath friends rich, but riches she hath none,
Nor none can her hands get to live upon.
This widow is very rich and her friends bare,
And both these for love to wed with me fond are.
And both would I wed, the better and the wurse,
The tone for her person, the tother for her purse :
They wooe not my substance, but my selfe they wooe,
Goods have I none and small good can I dooe.
On this poore maide, her rich friends, I cleerly know,
(So she wedde where they will), great gifts wil bestow,
But with them all I am so far from faver,
That she shall sure have no grote, if I have her ;
And I shall have as little all my friends sweare,
Except I follow them to wedde elswhere.
The poore friends of this rich widow beare no sway,
But wed her and win wealth, when I will I may.
Now which of these twaine is like to be deerest,
In paine or pleasure to sticke to me neerest ?

The depth of all doubts with you to consither,
The sense of the sayd proverbe sendeth me hither,
The best bargaine of both quickly to have skand,
For one of them think I to make out of hand.

Chapter II.

RIEND, (quoth I), welcome, and with right
good will,
I will as I can your minde herein fulfill.
And two things I see in you, that shew you wise,
First in wedding, ere ye wed to aske advise.
The second, your yeares being yong it appeares,
Ye regard yet good proverbs of old ferne yeares:
And as ye ground your tale upon one of them,
Furnish me this tale with everychone of them,
Such as may fitly fall in minde to dispose.
Agreed, (quoth he); then, (quoth I), first this disclose,
Have you to this old widow, or this yong mayd,
Any words of assurance ere this tyme sayd?
Nay in good faith, said he. Well then, (said I),
I will be plaine with you, and may honestly;
And plainly too speake, I like you, (as I sayd),

In two fore told things, but a third haue I wayd,

Not so much to be liked, as I can deeme,

Which is, in your wedding, your haste too extreeme.

The best and worst thing to man for this life,

Is good or ill choosing his good or ill wife.

I meane not onely of bodie good or bad,

But of all things meet or unmeete to be had,

Such as at any time by any meanes may,

Betweene man and wife, love encrease or decay.

Where this ground in any head gravely grateth,

All firie haste to wed, it soone rebateth.

Some things that provoke yong men to wed in haste,

Show after wedding, that *haste maketh waste.*

When *time hath turnd white sugar to white salt,*

Then such folke see, *soft fire mak'th sweet malt,*[1]

---

[1] *Soft fire mak'th sweet malt.*

Nicholas. O maister Philip, forbeare ; you must not leape over the stile before you come at it ; haste makes waste ; soft fire makes sweet malt ; not too far for falling ; there's no hast to hang true men.

Philip. Father, we ha'te, ye see, we ha'te. Now will I see if my memorie will serve for some proverbs, too. O,—a painted cloath were as well worth a shilling as a theefe worth a halter.— *Two Angry Women of Abington,* 1599.

> Hold, hold, quoth Hudibras, soft fire,
> They say, does make sweet malt, good Squire,
> *Festina lente,* not too fast ;
> For haste (the proverb says) makes waste.
>
> *Hudibras.*

And that deliberation doth men assist,

Before they 'wed to *beware of had I wist.*[2]

And then their timely wedding doth cleerely appeere

That they were *early up, and never the neere.*

And once their hastie heate a little controlde,

Then perceive they well, *hot love soone colde.*[3]

And when hastie witles mirth is mated weele,

Good to be merie and wise,[4] they thinke and feele.

---

[2] *Beware of had I wist.*

A common exclamation of regret occurring in Spenser, Harrington and the older writers. " Beware of had-I-wist " is the title of a poem in the *Paradise of Dainty Devices*, 1578 ; and in *Witt's Recreation*, 1654, the expression is rhymed upon in an epitaph on one Walter Moon :—

> Here lies Wat Moon, that great tobacconist,
> Who dye'd too soon for lack of had-I-wist.

An earlier instance of the application of this phrase is found in the *Towneley Mysteries*, circa 1420 :—

> Be welle war of wedyng, and thynk in youre thought
> " Had I wist " is a thyng it servys of nought.

The term could not have been uncommon so late as 1827, in which year a Mr. Jeffries Taylor (*Old English Sayings Expoundea*) wrote a moral essay with the proverb as its title.

[3] *Hot love soone colde.*

> Dowghter, in this I can thinke none oother
> But that it is true thys proverbe old,
> Hastye love is soone hot and soone cold !
> > *Play of Wyt and Science,* circa 1540.

[4] *Good to be merie and wise.*

Touchstone. Did I gaine my wealth by ordinaries ? no ; by

Haste in wedding some man thinketh his own availe,
When haste proveth *a rod made for his own taile.*
And when he is well *beaten with his owne rod,*[5]
Then seeth he haste and wisedome things far od ;
And that in all, or most things, wisht at neede,
Most times he seeth, *the more haste the lesse speede.*
In lesse things than wedding, haste shew'th hastie mās
        foe,
So that *the hastie man never wanteth woe.*[6]
These sage said sawes if ye take so profound,
As ye take that by which ye tooke your ground,
Then finde ye grounded cause by these now here told
In haste to wedding your haste to withold.

---

changing of gold? no. I hired me a little shop, fought low,
tooke small gaine, kept no debt booke, garnished my shop,
for want of plate, with good wholesome, thriftie sentences ;
as, " Touchstone, keepe thy shoppe, and thy shoppe will
keepe thee." " Light gaines make heavie purses." " 'Tis good
to be merry and wise."—*Eastward Hoe,* 1605, by CHAPMAN,
MARSTON, and BEN JONSON.

[5] *Beaten with his owne rod.*

> —— don fust
> C'on kint sovent est-on batu.
>   *Roman du Renart,* circa 1300.

[6] *The hastie man never wanteth woe.*

Mistress Touchstone. Thou wert afire to be a ladie, and now
your ladiship and you may both blowe at the cole, for aught I
know. " Selfe doe, selfe have." " The hastie man never
wanteth woe " they say.—*Eastward Hoe,* act v. sc. I.

And though they seeme wives for you never so fit,
Yet let not harmfull haste so far out run your wit:
But that ye harke to heare all the whole summe
That may please or displease you in time to cumme.
Thus by these lessons ye may learne good cheape
In wedding and all things to *looke ere ye leape.*[1]
Ye have even now well over lookte me, (quoth he),
And leapt very nie me too.   For I agree
That these sage sayings doe weightily way
Against hast in all thing, but I am at bay.
By other parables of like weighty weight,
Which hast me to wedding, as yee shall heare streight.

---

[1] *Looke ere ye leape.*

In *Tottel's Miscellany*, 1557 ; and in *Five Hundred Points of Good Husbandry*, 1573, by THOMAS TUSSER.

Chapter III.

E that will not when he may,
　　When he would he shall have nay.[8]
　　Beautie or riches the tone of the twaine
Now may I choose, and which me list obtaine.
And if we determine me this mayde to take,
And then tract of time traine her me to forsake,
Then my beautifull mariage lieth in the dike;
And never for beautie shall wed the like.
Now if we award me this widow to wed,
And that I drive off time, till time she be ded,
Then farewell riches, *the fat is in the fire,*[9]
And never shall I to like riches aspire.
And a thousand fold would it grieve me more
That she in my faulte should die an houre before

---

[8] *He that will not, &c.*
In Burton's *Anatomy of Melancholy,* 1621:—
　　　　He that will not when he may,
　　　　When he will he shall have nay.

[9] *The fat is in the fire.*
Phy. Faith, Doricus, thy braine boils; keele it, keele it, or all the fatt's in the fire.—Marston's *What You Will,* 1607.

Than one minute after ; than haste must provoke
When the pigge is profferd to hold up the poke ;
When the Sunne shineth make hay ; which is to say,
. Take time when time comth, lest time steale away.
And one good lesson to this purpose I pike
From the smith's forge, *when th' iron is hot, strike.*[10]
The sure Seaman seeth, *the tide tarieth no man,*[11]
And long delayes or absence somewhat to skan,

---

[10] *When th' iron is hot, strike.*

Birdlime. Strike whilst the iron is hot. A woman, when there
be roses in her cheeks, cherries on her lips, civet in her breath,
ivory in her teeth, lilies in her hand, and liquorice in her heart,
why, she's like a play : if new, very good company ; but if stale,
like old Jeronimo, go by, go by, therefore, as I said before, strike.
Besides, you must think that the commodity of beauty was not
made to lie dead upon any young woman's hands : if your husband
have given up his cloak, let another take measure of you in his
jerkin ; for as the cobbler in the night-time walks with his lantern,
the merchant and the lawyer with his link, and the courtier with
his torch, so every lip has its lettuce to himself : the lob has his
lass, the collier his dowdy, the western-man his punk, the student
his nun in Whitefriars, the puritan his sister, and the lord his
lady ; which worshipful vocation may fall upon you, if you'll but
strike whilst the iron is hot.—WEBSTER'S *Westward Hoe,* 1607.

Messieurs, ce pendant que le fer est chauld il le fault battre.
RABELAIS, ii. 31.

[11] *The tide tarieth no man.*

In a poem by Robert Southwell, a work in every respect much
above the average of the didactic poetry of that day, the proverbial saying is introduced into a carefully wrought stanza :—

Hoist up saile while gale doth last,
Tide and wind stay no man's pleasure ;

Since *that one will not another will,*

Delayes in wooers must needes their speede spill.

And touching absence, the full account who somthe

Shall see, *as fast as one goeth another comthe.*

Time is tickle; and *out of sight, out of minde;* [12]

Than catch and hold while I may, *fast binde fast finde.* [13]

    Seeke not time, when time is past,
      Sober speed is wisedome's leisure ;
    After wits are dearely bought,
    Let thy fore wit guide thy thought.

The poem continues :—

    Time weares all his lockes before,
      Take thou hold upon his forehead ;
    When he flies, he turnes no more,
      And behinde his scalpe is naked.
    Workes adjourn'd have many stayes
    Long demurres breed new delayes.

    Seeke thy salve whilst sore is greene,
      Festered wounds aske deeper launcing ;
    After-cures are seldome seene,
      Often sought, scarce ever chancing.
    Time and place gives best advice.
    Out of season out of price.

                    St. Peter's Complaint, 1595.

[12] *Out of sight, out of minde.*

The saying has been traced to the *De Imitatione Christi,* by Thomas à Kempis, written circa 1450 :—" Cum autem sublatus fuerit ab oculis, cito etiam transit a mente." It occurs, however, prior to this in an early English fragment :—

      " Fer from e3e, fer from herte "
      Quoth Hendyng.

            Proverbs of Hendyng, ms. circa 1320.

[13] *Fast binde fast finde.*

Shylock.   Well, Jessica, go in ;

Blame mee not to hast for feare myne eye bee blerde.

And thereby the fat cleane flitte fro my berde.

Where wooers hop in and out, long time may bring

Him that hoppeth best, at last to have the ring.

I hopping without for a ring of a rush,

And *while I* at length debate and *beate the bush,*

There shall steppe in *other men* and *catch the burdes.*[14]

And by long time lost in many vaine wurdes,

Betweene these two wives make sloth speed confound,

While *betweene two stooles my taile goe to the ground.*[15]

Perhaps, I will return immediately ;
Do, as I bid you,
Shut doors after you ; Fast bind, fast find ;
A proverb never stale in thrifty mind.
Merchant of Venice, ii. 5.

Wherefore a plaine bargain is best, and in bargaines making ; fast bind, fast find.—*Jests of Scogin,* 1565.

[14] *While I . . . . beate the bush, &c.*

I beat the bush, and others catch the bird,
Reason exclaimes and sweares my hap is hard.
Philochasander and Elanira, 1599, by HENRY PETTOWE.

It is this proverb which Henry the Fifth is reported to have uttered at the siege of Orleans, when the citizens, besieged by the English, declared themselves willing to yield the town to the Duke of Burgundy, who was in the English camp. " Shall I beat the bush, and another take the bird ?" said King Henry. The Duke was so offended that he withdrew his troops and concluded a peace.

[15] *Betweene two stooles, &c.*

A proverb found in a French manuscript of the 14th century :—

A grant folie entent
Qui deus choses enprent

By this, since we see slouth must breed a scab.

Best sticke to the tone out of hand, *hab or nab.*

Thus all your proverbs inveying against hast,

Be answered with proverbs plaine and promptly plast,

Whereby to purpose all this no further fits,

But to shew, *so many heads so many wits.*[16]

Which shew, as surely in all that they all tell,

That in my wedding I may even as well

Tary too long and thereby come to late,

As come too soone by hast in any rate ;

And prove this proverbe as the wordes thereof goe,

Hast or sloth herein woorke neither welth nor woe.

E nule ne acheive ;
Savey hi l'en dessert :
L'une par autre pert
E sei meismes greves.
Entre deux arcouns chet cul à terre.
Les Proverbes del Vilain, MS. Bodleian, circa 1300.
Is afterwards used by RABELAIS, *Gargantua*, liv. i. c. ii.
" S'asseoir entre deux selles le cul à terre."

[16] *So many heads so many wits.*

For amonge feaders are alwayes sondry appetytes, and in great assemblyes of people, dyvurse, and varyaunt judgements ; as the saynge is, so many heades, so many wyttes.—*Godly Meditacyon of the Christen Sowle*, by QUEEN ELIZABETH, 1548.

Phylautus. Ah, sirha, I see wel the olde proverbe is true, which saith : so many men so many mindes.—GASCOIGNE'S *Glasse of Government*, 1575.

Quot homines tot sententiæ.
TERENCE.

Be it far or nie, *wedding is destiny,*

And hanging likewise [17], sayth the proverbe, sayd I.

Then wedde or hang, (quoth he), what helpeth in the
      whole,

To hast or to hang aloofe, *happy man happy dole.*[18]

Ye deale this dole, (quoth I), out at a wrong dur,

For destiny in this case doth not so stur

Agaynst mans indeavour, but man may direct

His will, fore provision to worke or neglect.

But to shew that quick wedding may bring good
      speed,

Somewhat to purpose your proverbs prove indeede.

Howbeit, whether they counterpaise or outway

The proverbes which I before them did lay,

---

[17] *Wedding is destiny and hanging likewise.*

An earlier mention of the saying, " Hanging and wiving go by destiny," is found in the *Schole-hous for Women*, 1541. In 1558, a ballad was licensed with the title "The Proverbe is true yᵗ Weddynge is destinyē."

[18] " Happy man be your dole" was an exclamation implying a wish for success to any one engaging in a contest or entering upon an undertaking.

> —— Mine honest friend,
> Will you take eggs for money?
> *Mam.* No, my lord, I'll fight.
> *Leo.* You will? why, happy man be his dole!
> > *Winter's Tale*, i. 2.

> Happy man be his dole that misses her.
> > *Grim the Collier of Croydon.*

The trial thereof we will *lay a water*,[19]
Til we trye more.   For trying of which mater,
Declare all commodities ye can devise,
That by those two weddings to you can rise.

CHAPTER IV.

 WILL, (quoth he), in both these cases
streight show
What things, (as I thinke), to me by them
will grow.
And where my love began, there begin will I
With this maide, the peece peereles in mine eie,
Whom I so favour, and she so favoureth me,
That halfe a death to us tis asunder to be.
Affection each to other doth us so move,
That welny without food we could live by love ;
For be I right sad or right sicke from her sight,
Her presence absenteth all maladies quight ;
Which sheweth that the great ground in mariage,

---

[19] *Lay a water.*

If he had broke his arme. . . . . either Apollo must have played
Bonesetter, or every occupation beene laide a water.—GOSSON'S
Schoole of Abuse, 1579.

Standeth upon liking the parties personage.

And then of old proverbs, in opening the pack,

One shew'th me openly, *in love is no lack ;*

No lack of liking, but lack of living.

Nay lack in love, (quoth I), may breed its chieving.

Well as to that, (said he), harke this one thing,

What time I lack not her, I lack nothing.

But though we have nought, nor nought we can get,

God never send'th mouth but he sendeth meat :

And *a hard beginning makth a good ending :*

In space comth grace and this further amending,

Seldome comth the better,[20] and *like will to like :*[1]

God send'th cold after clothes ;[2] and this I pike,

She, by lack of substance, seeming but a sparke,

Steinth yet the stoutest : for *a legge of a larke*

---

[20] *Seldome comth the better.*

This change is like to the rest of worldy chaunges, that is, from the better to the worse : For as the Proverb sayth : Seldome coms the better.—*English Courtier and Country Gentleman,* 1586.

[1] *Like will to like.*

—— like to like, ye ken—it's a proverb never fails ; and ye are baith a pair o' the deevil's peats, I trow—hard to ken whilk deserves the hottest corner o' his ingleside.—*Heart of Midlothian.*

[2] *God send'th cold after clothes.*

" Dieu donne le froid selon la robbe," is the French form of this proverb, found in *Les Prémices,* 1594, by HENRY ESTIENNE.

C

Is better than is the bodie of ä kight ; [3]

And home is homely, though it be poore in sight.

These proverbs for this part shew such a flourish,

And then this partie doth delight to nourish ;

That much is my bow bent to shoot at these markes,

And kill feare ; *when the skie falth we shall have Larkes.* [4]

All perils that fall may, who feareth they fall shall,

Shall so feare all things that he shall let fall all ;

And be *more frayd then hurt,* if the things be done ;

Feare may force a man to *cast beyond the moone.* [5]

Who hopeth in Gods helpe, his helpe cannot start,

Nothing is impossible to a willing hart.

And will may winne my hart herein to consent

---

[3] *A legge of a larke, &c.*

Gyrtrude. I would not change husbands with my sister ; I. "The legge of a larke is better than the body of a kite."
Mistress Touchstone. Know that ; but—
Gyrtrude. What, sweet mother, what ?
Mistress Touchstone. It's but ill food when nothing's left but the claw.—*Eastward Hoe,* by CHAPMAN, MARSTON, and BEN JONSON, 1605.

[4] *When the skie falth we shall have Larkes.*

Si les nues tomboyent esperoyt prendre les alouettes.—RABE-LAIS, *Gargantua.*

[5] "To cast beyond the moon" is a proverbial phrase, in frequent use by the old writers to signify attempting impossibilities.

But oh, I talk of things impossible
And cast beyond the moon.
A Woman Kill'd with Kindness, 1607.

To take all things as it comth, and be content.
And here is, (quoth he), in marying of this mayde,
For courage and commoditie all myne ayde.
Well sayd, (quoth I), but a while keepe me in quench,
All this case, as touching this poore young wench.
And now declare your whole consideration,
What maner thinges draw your imagination,
Toward your wedding of this widow rich and olde?
That shall ye, (quoth he), out of hand have told.

Chapter V.

HIS Widow being foule and of favour ill,
In good behaviour can very good skill:
Pleasantly spoken, and a very good wit;
And at her table when we together sit,
I am well served; we fare of the best.
The meate good and holsome and holsomely drest:
Sweet and soft lodging, and thereof great shift;
This felt and seene with all implementes of thrift,
Of plate and money, such cupboordes and coffers,
And that without penie I may win these proffers.
Than covetyse bearing Venus bargayne backe,
Praysing this bargayne sayth, *better leave then lacke.*

And greedines to draw desire to her lore,

Saith, that the wise man sayth, *store is no sore.*

Who hath many Pease may put the mo in the pot;

Of two ils chose the least,[6] while choise lyeth in lot.

Since lacke is an ill, as ill as man may have;

To provide for the worst, while the best it selfe save;

Resty welth wilth me [7] this widow to winne,

To *let the world wagge,*[8] and take *mine ease in myne Inne.*[9]

He must needes swim that is hold up by the chinne;[10]

---

[6] *Of two ils chose the least.*

> Of harmes two the lesse is for to cheese.
> > CHAUCER, *Troilus and Cressida.*

[7] *Resty welth wilth me, i. e.,* rusty wealth compels me, &c. Reastie or rusty, in the sense of rancid, is generally applied by the old writers to provisions.

> From rusty bacon, and ill rosted eeles,
> And from a madding wit that runnes on wheels.
> > *Witt's Recreations,* 1634.

[8] *Let the world wagge.*

An exclamation almost identical with this occurs in the old morality, *The iiii. Elements,* 1510; and again more humorously in Shakespeare's *Taming of the Shrew.*

Sly. Y'are a baggage; the Slies are no rogues; Look in the chronicles, we came in with Richard Conqueror. Therefore, paucas pallabris; let the world slide.

[9] *Mine ease in myne Inne.*

Falstaff. Shall I not take mine ease in mine inn, but I shall have my pocket picked?—I *Henry IV.* iii. 2.

[10] *He must needes swim that is hold up by the chinne.*

> In *Scogin's Jests,* 1565.

He laugth that winth.[11]   And this threed finer to spinne,

Mayster promotion sayth, make this substance sure ;

If riches bring ones portly countenance in ure,[12]

Then shalt thou *rule the rost* [13] all round about ;

And better to rule than to be ruled by the rout.

It is sayd, be it better be it wurse,

Doe you after him that beareth the purse.

Thus be I by this, once *le senior de graunde,*

Many that command me, I shall commaunde.

And also I shall to revenge former hurtes,

Hold their noses to grinstone, and sit on their skurtes,

That erst sate on myne.   And riches may make

Frendes many wayes.   Thus *better to give then to take.*

And to make carnall appetite content,

---

[11] *He laugth that winth.*

The reverse side of this proverb is the more common.

Give losers leave to talk.

TAYLOR'S *Arrant Thiefe,* 1622.

I, I, wele give loosers leave to talke : it is no matter what *sic probo* and his pennilesse companions prate, whilst we have the gold in our coffers.—NASH'S *Pierce Penilesse,* 1592.

[12] *Ure,* an Anglo-Norman word equivalent to the French *heure,* of which word it is a corruption.   This is one of the latest instances of the application of the word, which was current in the time of Chaucer.

[13] *Rule the rost.*

But at the pleasure of me

That ruleth the roste alone.

SKELTON'S *Colyn Cloute,* circa 1518.

Reason laboreth will, to win wil's consent,

To take lacke of beauty but as *an eie sore*,[14]

The fayre and the foule by darke are like store.

When all candles bee out all cattes be gray ;

All things are then of one colour, as who say :

And this proverbe sayth, for quenching hot desire,

Foule water as sone as fayre will quench hot fire.

Where giftes be given freely, East, West, North or
        South,

No man ought to looke a given horse in the mouth.[15]

And though her mouth be foule, shee hath a faire taile ;

I conster this text, as is most my availe.

In want of white teeth and yellow hayres to behold,

Shee flourisheth in white silver and yellow gold.

What though she be toothles and *bald as a coote ?*

Her substance is shoote ankre whereat I shoote.

---

[14] *An eie sore.*

> Quod the Barbour, but a lytell eye sore.
> > *Mery Jests of the Wyddow Edyth*, 1525.

[15] *No man ought to looke a given horse in the mouth.*

This proverb occurs in *Vulgaria Stambrigi*, printed by Wynkyn
de Worde and Peter Trevaris, circa 1510.

> " A gyven hors may not be loked in the tethe."

Archbishop Trench (*Proverbs and their Lessons*) observes of
this saying :—

" I will not pretend to say how old it may be, but it is certainly
as old as Jerome, a Latin father of the fourth century ; who when
some found fault with certain writings of his, replies with a tart-

Take a payne for a pleasure all wise men can ;

What, *hungry dogges will eate durty puddinges*, man ? [16]

And here I conclude, (quoth he,) all that I know,

By this old widow, what good to me may grow.

CHAPTER VI.

E have, (quoth I), in these conclusions found
Sundry things that very saverly sound ;
And both these .long cases, being well
viewde,

In one short question we may well inclewde ;

Which is, whether best or woorst be to be ledde

With riches, without love or beauty, to wedde ;

Or with beauty without riches for love.

This question, (quoth he), inquir'th all that I move.

It doth so, (said I), and is neerly couched,

But th' answere will not so briefly be touched ;

---

ness which he could occasionally exhibit, that they were voluntary
on his part, free-will offerings, and with this quoted the proverb,
that it did not behove to look a gift horse in the mouth. And
before it comes to us, we meet it once more in one of the rhymed
Latin verses, which were such great favourites in the middle ages.

Si quis dat mannos, ne quære in dentibus annos.

[16] *Hungry dogges, &c.*

There is another proverb which declares that a hungry man
will eat anything, except Suffolk cheese.

And your selfe, to length it, taketh direct trade.[17]
For all reasons that I have yet made,
Yee seeme more to seeke reasons how to contend,
Than to the counsell of mine to condiscend.
And to be playne, as I must with my frend,
I perfectly feele even *at my fingers end ;*
So hard is your hand set on your halfpeny,[18]
That my reasoning your reason setteth naught by.
But reason for reason, yee so stifly lay,
By proverbe for proverbe, that with you doe way,
That reason onely shall herein nought move you
To heare more then speake, wherefore I will prove you
With reason assisted by experience,
Which myself saw, not long since nor farre hence,
In a matter so like this fashiond in frame,
That none can be liker, it seemeth even the same.
And in the same, as your selfe shall espy,
Each sentence soothed with a proverbe welny.
And at ende of the same, yee shall cleerly see,

---

[17] *Trade, i.e.* a way, a means.
    Long did I serve this lady,
  Long was my travel, long my trade to win her.
      MASSINGER, *Very Woman.*
[18] *So hard is your hand set on your halfpeny.*
Ri. Dromio, looke heere, now is my hand on my half-peny.
Half. Thou liest, thou hast not a farthing to lay thy hands on.
    Mother Bombie, by JOHN LYLY, 1594.

How this short question shortly answered may bee.
Ye may, (quoth he), now yee shoote nie the pricke;[19]
Practise in all, above all toucheth the quicke.
Proofe upon practise, must take hold more sure
Then any reasoning by gesse can procure.
If ye bring practise in place, without fabling,
I will banish both hast and busie babling.
And yet that promise to performe is mickell,
For in this case my tong must oft tickell.
Ye know well it is, as telth us this old tale,
Meete that a man be at his owne brydale.[20]
If he wive well, (quoth I), meete and good it were ;
Or els as good for him another were there.
But for this your bridale, I meane not in it,
That silence shall suspend your speech every whit.
But in these mariages which ye here meve,
Since this tale containeth the counsell I can geve,
I would see your eares attend with your tong ;
For advyse in both these weddinges old and yong.

---

[19] *Pricke, i.e.* the centre of a target. The word was used to signify any particular spot ; in the old copies of Euclid it is printed where we now read " point."

[20] *Brydale,* a wedding festivity.

There were bride-ales, church-ales, clerk-ales, give-ales, lamb-ales, leet-ales, Midsummer-ales, Scot-ales, Whitsun-ales, and several more.—BRAND'S *Popular Antiquities.*

In which hearing, tyme seene when and what to talk
When your tong tickleth, at will let it walke.
And in these brydales, to the reasons of ours,
Marke mine experience in this case of yours.

CHAPTER VII.

WITHIN few yeares past, from London no
      far way,
    Where I and my wife with our poore hous-
      hold lay:
Two yong men were abyding, whom to discrive,
Were I in portraying persons dead or alive,
As cunning and as quicke, to touch then at full,
As in that feat I am ignorant and dull;
Never could I paynt their pictures to allow,
More lively than to paynt the picture of you.
And as your three persons shew one similitude,
So shew you three one in all things to be viewd.
Lykewise a widow and a mayde there did dwell;
Alyke, lyke the widow and mayde ye of tell.
The frendes of them foure in every degree,
Standing in state as the frendes of you three.
Those two men each other so hasted or taried,
That those two women on one day they maryed.

Into two houses, which next my house did stand,
The one on the right, the other on the left hand,
Both Bridegromes bad mee ; I could doe none other,
But dyne with the tone, and suppe with the tother.
He that wedded this Widow rich and olde,
And also she favoured me so, that they would
Make me dyne or suppe once or twyce in a weeke.
This poore young man and his make,[1] being to seeke
As oft where they might eate or drinke, I them bad,
Were I at home, to such pittaunce as I had.
Which common conference such confidence wrought
In them to me that deed, woord, ne welny thought
Chaunced among them, what ever it were,
But one of the foure brought it to mine eare.
Whereby betweene these twaine and their two wives,
Both for wealth and woe, I knew all their four lives.
And since the matter is much intricate,
Betweene side and side, I shall here separate
All matters on both sides, and then sequestrate
Th' one side, while th' other be full reherst in rate,

---

[1] *His make, i. e.* his wife.

> All your parishoners,
> As well your laïcks, as your quiristers,
> Had need to keep to their warm feather-beds,
> If they be sped of loves ; this is no season
> To seek new makes in.
>   BEN JONSON, *Tale of a Tub*, i. 1.

As for your understanding may best stand ;

And this young poore couple shall come first in hand.

Who, the day of wedding and after a while,

Could not looke each on other but they must smile,

As a whelpe for wantonnes in and out whippes,

So plaide these twaine, *as mery as three chippes.*

Yea, there was God, (quoth he), when all is doone.

Abyde, (quoth I), it was yet but hony moone ;

The blacke oxe had not trode on his nor her foote ; [2]

But ere this braunch of blisse could reach any roote,

The flowers so faded that in fifteene weekes,

A man might espye the change in their cheekes.

Both of this poore wretch and his wife this poore
          wench,

Their faces tolde toies that *Totnam was turnd French.*[3]

And all their light laughing turnd and translated

---

[2] *The blacke oxe, &c.*

This proverb, meaning to fall into decrepitude or experience
misfortune, occurs again in Lyly's *Sapho and Phao*, 1584:

Venus waxeth old: and then she was a pretie wench, when Juno
was a young wife ; now crowes foote is on her eye, and the black
oxe hath trod on her foot.

[3] *Totnam was turnd French.*

A phrase implying a great alteration.   It takes its origin from
the migration of a number of French workmen to this locality
early in the reign of Henry VIII.   Their competition provoked
the jealousy of English mechanics, and resulted in disturbances
in the streets of London on May-day, 1517.

Into sad sighing ; all mirth was amated.[4]

And one morning timely he tooke in hand

To make to my house *a sleeveless errand,*[5]

Hauking upon me, his minde herein to breake,

Which I would not see till he began to speake,

Praying me to heare him ; and I sayd, I would.

Wherewith this that followeth forthwith he tould.

---

[4] *Amated,* dismayed.

> That I amazed and amated am,
> To see Great Brittaine turn'd to Amsterdam.
>   TAYLOR'S *Mad Fashions,* 1642.

[5] *A sleeveless errand.*

The origin of the word sleeveless, in the sense of unprofitable, has defied the most careful philological research. I would suggest that the phrase originated in the mediæval custom of favoured knights wearing the sleeve of their mistress as a mark of favour ; such aspirants as failed to obtain the badge being dubbed as sleeveless. Spenser writes—" Sir Launcelot wore the sleive of the faire maide of Asteloth in a tourney, whereat queene Guenever was much displeased." The word sleeveless is frequently found allied to other substantives. Bishop Hall speaks of the "sleeveless tale of transubstantiation," and Milton writes of a "sleeveless reason." Chaucer uses it in the "Testament of Love," and three centuries afterwards its place in popular estimation appears from a passage in Addison's "Spectator:"—"My landlady quarrelled with him for sending every one of her children on a sleeveless errand, as she calls it."

Chapter VIII.

AM now driven, (quoth he), for ease of my
hart,
To you, to utter part of mine inward smart.
And the matter concerneth my wife and mee,
Whose fathers and mothers long since dead bee,
But uncles, with auntes and cosins have wee,
Divers rich on both sides, so that we did see
If we had wedded, each, where each kindred would,
Neither of us had lackt either silver or gold.
But never could suite on either side obtaine
One peny to the one wedding of us twaine.
And since our one marying, or marring, day,
Where any of them see us they shrinke away,
Solemnly swearing such as may give ought,
Whyle they and we live, of them we get right nought.
Nor nought have we, nor no way ought can we get,
Saving by borrowing til we be in det,
So far that no man any more will us lend,
Whereby for lacke we both be *at our wittes end.*
Whereof no wonder since the end of our good,

And beginning of our charge together stood.
But *wit is never good till it be bought.*[6]
Howbeit when bought wits to best price be brought,
Yet is *one good fore-wit woorth two after wits.*
This *payeth me home* loe and ful moe folly hits,
For had I lookt afore with indifferent eye,
Though hast had made me thrust never so dry,
Yet to drowne this drought this must I needes thinke,
As I would needes brewe so must I needes drinke.[7]
The drinke of my bride cup I should have forborne,
Till temperance had tempred the tast beforne.
I see now and shall see while I am alive,
Who wedth ere he be wise shall die ere he thrive.
I sing now in this fact *factus est repente,*
Now myne eyes be open I doe repent me,
He that will sell lawne before he can fold it,
He shall repent him before he have sold it.

---

[6] *Wit is never good, &c.*

Stationers could not live, if men did not beleeve the old saying, that Wit bought is better then Wit taught.—*Conceits, Clinches, Flashes and Whimzies,* 1639.

[7] *As I would needes brewe, so must I needes drinke.*

One of a whole family of proverbs pointing out the connection between the cause and the result.

If you have browen wel, you shal drinke the better.
WODROEPHE'S *Spared Houres of a Souldier,* 1623.

Some bargains deare bought, *good cheape*[8] would be
    sold ;

No man loveth his fetters, be they made of gold.[9]

Were I loose from the lovely linkes of my chaine,

I would not daunce in such faire fetters againe,

In house to kepe houshold, *when folkes will needes wed,*

Moe thinges belong then foure bare legges in a bed.[10]

I reckened my wedding a suger sweete spice,

But *reckeners without their host must recken twice.*[11]

And although it were sweet for a weeke or twaine,

Sweete meate will have sowre sawce, I see now plaine.

Continuall penury, which I must take,

---

[8] *Good cheape.*

Cheap = market ; good cheap = bon marché.

He buys other men's cunning good cheap in London, and sels
it deare in the country.—DECKER'S *Belman's Night-walks.*

[9] *No man loves his fetters, &c.*

  Who would weare fetters though they were all of gold ?
  Or to be sicke, though his faint browes,
  For wearing Night-cap, wore a Crown.
               Famous History of Sir Thomas Wyatt,
               1607, *by* WEBSTER.

[10] *Foure bare legges in a bed.*

Furthermore it shall be lawful for him that marries without
money to find four bare legs in a bed : and he that is too pro-
digal in spending, shall die a beggar by the statute.—*Pennilesse
Parliament of Threadbare Poets,* 1608.

[11] *Reckeners without their host must recken twice.*

      " Comptoit sans son hoste."
              RABELAIS, *Gargantua.*

Telth me, *better eie out then alway ake.*

Boldly and blindly I ventred on this,

How be it, *who so bold as blinde Bayard is ?*[12]

And herein to blame any man, then should I rave,

For I did it my selfe : and *selfe doe, selfe have.*[13]

But a *day after the faire,* commeth this remorse

For releife ; for though *it be a good horse*

That never stumbleth,[14] what praise can that avouch

To jades that breake their neckes at first trip or touch ?

And before this my first foile or breakneck fall,

Subtilly like a sheepe, though[t] I, I shall

Cut my cote after my cloth[15] when I have her.

---

[12] *Who so bold as blinde Bayard is ?*

This proverb is applied where persons act without consideration or reflection. Its antiquity is apparent from its occurring in *The Vision of Piers the Ploughman,* 1362, and in CHAUCER'S *Canterbury Tales.* The word "bayard" originally meant a grey horse, a meaning which was afterwards extended to denote a horse in general; and Skelton mentions a description of horse-loaf called bayard's bun. It will be remembered that Rinaldo's horse in Ariosto's great work is called Baiardo.

[13] *Selfe doe, selfe have.*

Yea, said shee, selfe do, selfe have : many a man thinketh to doe another man a shrewd turne and it turneth oftimes to his owne selfe.—*Mery Tales of the Mad Men of Gotham,* circa 1450.

[14] *A good horse that never stumbleth.*

A good horse that trippeth not once in a journey.—*Three Proper and Wittie Familiar Letters,* 1580.

[15] *Cut my cote after my cloth.*

A relic of the Sumptuary Laws, one of the earliest allusions to

D

But *now I can smell, nothing hath no saver.*
I am taught to know, in *more hast then good speede,*
How Judicare came into the Creede.
My carefull wife in one corner weepeth in care,
And I in an other ; the purse is threed-bare.
This corner of our care, (quoth he), I you tell,
To crave therein your comfortable counsell.

Chapter IX.

AM sory (quoth I), of your poverty ;
And more sory, that I cannot succour yee.
If yee sturre your neede myne almes to stur,
Then of troth *yee beg at a wrong mans dur.*
I come to begge nothing of you, (quoth hee),
Save your advice, which may my best way bee ;

---

which occurs 1530, in the interlude of *Godly Queene Hestor,* where
Pride complains that no one can wear gay apparel since Haman
has bought up all the cloth.

You, with your fraternitie, in these latter dayes, cannot be content to shape your Coate according to your Cloth.—*A Health to
the Gentlemanly Profession of Servingmen,* 1598.

How to win present salve for this present sore.
I am like th' ill surgeon, (sayd I), without store
Of good playsters.   Howbeit such as they are,
Yee shall have the best I have.   But first declare
Where yours and your wives rich kinsfolkes do dwell.
Envyronned about us, (quoth hee), which sheweth
     well,
The neer to the church, the further from God.[16]
Most part of them dwell within a thousand rod ;
And yet shall wee *catch a hare with a taber,*[17]
As soone as catch ought of them, and rather.
Ye play coleprophet, (quoth I), who tak'th in hand,
To know his answere before he do his errand.
What should I to them, (quoth hee), fling or flitte ?
An unbidden guest knoweth not where to sit.
I am cast at cartes arse ; some folke in lacke

---

[16] *The neer to the church, &c.*

Qui est près de l'église est souvent loin de Dieu.—*Les Proverbes Communs*, circa 1500.

[17] *Catch a hare with a taber.*

One day after the set of this comet men shall catch hares with tabers. . . . Such as are inclined to the dropsy may be cured if the phisitions know how : and if there be no great store of tempests, two halfe penny loves shall be solde for a penny in White-Chappell.   Chaucer's bookes shall this yeere prove more witty thin ever they were.—*Fearefull and Lamentable Effects of Two dangerous Comets.*   By SIMON SMEL-KNAVE, Student in Good Felowship, 1591.

Cannot prease : *a broken sleeve holdeth th' arme*
    backe ;[18]

And shame holdeth me backe, being thus forsaken.

Tush man, (quoth I), *shame is as it is taken.*

And shame take him that shame thinketh yee have
    none.

Unminded, unmoned ; goe *make your mone*

Till meate fall in your mouth ; will yee lye in bed,

Or sit still ? nay, hee *that gapeth till hee bee fed*

May fortune to fast and famish for honger.

Set forward, yee shall never labour yonger.

Well, (quoth hee), if I shall needes this viage make

With as good will as a Beare goth to the stake,

I will strayght waie anker, and hoise up sayle,

And thitherward hie me *in hast like a snayle,*

And home againe hitherward *quicke as a Bee ;*

Now for good lucke, *cast an old shooe after mee.*[19]

---

[18] *A broken sleeve holdeth th' arme backe.*
> It is a terme with John and Jacke,
> Broken sleeve draweth arme a backe.
>> *Parlament of Byrdes,* 1550.
> *Johphiel.* Reach forth your hand.
> *Meere Foole.* O sir, a broken sleeve
> Keepes the arm back, as tis the proverbe.
>> *The Fortunate Isles,* 1624, *by* BEN JONSON.

[19] *Cast an old shooe after mee.*
> Captain, your shoes are old, pray put 'em off,
> And let one fling 'em after us.
>> BEAUMONT AND FLETCHER, *Honest Man's Fortune.*

And first to myne uncle, brother to my father,
By suite, I will assay to winne some faver :
Who brought me up, and till my wedding was don,
Loved me not as his nephew, but as his son.
And his heire had I bin, had not this chaunced,
Of lands and goods which should me much avaunced.
Trudge, (quoth I), to him, and on your maribones
Crouch to the ground, and not so oft as ones
Speake any one woord him to contrary.
I can not tell that, (quoth he), by saint Mary ;
One ill woord axeth another, as folkes speake.
Well, (quoth I), *better is to bow then breake ;*[20]
It hurteth not the toung to giue faire woordes ;[1]
The rough net is not the best catcher of burdes.
Since ye can nought winne, if ye can not please,

---

[20] *Better is to bow then breake.*

Probably the earliest example of the use of this proverb is
that in *The Morale Proverbs of Cristyne* ; originally written in
French about the year 1390 and of which a verse translation
by Earl Rivers was printed by Caxton in 1478. The following
is the form in which it is found in the latter version : —

> Rather to bowe than breke is profitable,
> Humylite is a thing commendable.

[1] *It hurteth not the toung to geue fayre woordes.*

Gertrude. Come away, I say ; hunger drops out at his nose.
Goulding. O, madam, faire words never hurt the tongue.
  Eastward Hoe, 1605, by JONSON, CHAPMAN, and MARSTON.

Best is to suffer : for *of suffrance comth ease.*[2]
Cause causeth, (quoth he) ; and as cause causeth me,
So will I doo.   And with this away went he.
Yet whether his wife should goe with him or no,
He sent her to me to know ere he would goe.
Whereto I sayde, I thought best he went alone ;
And you, (quoth I), to goe streight as he is gone,
Among your kinsfolke likewise, if they dwell nye.
Yes, (quoth she), all round about even hereby.
Namely, an aunt, my mother's sister, who well,
(Since my mother died), brought me up from the shell ;
And much would have geven me, had my wedding
        growne
Upon her fansie, as it grewe upon myne owne.
And in likewise myne uncle, her husband, was
A father to me.   Well, (quoth I), let pas :
And if your husbande will his assent graunt,
Goe, he to his uncle, and you to your aunt.
Yes, this assent he graunteth before, (quoth she) ;
For he ere this thought this the best way to be ;
But of these two thinges he would determine none
Without aid.   For *two heads are better then one.*
With this wee departed, shee to her husband,
And I to dinner to them on th' other hand.

---

[2] *Of suffrance comth ease.*
    Ile give a proverbe—Sufferance giveth ease.
        MARSTON'S *What you Will,* 1607.

CHAPTER X.

WHEN dinner was done I came home agayne
    To attend on the returne of these twayne;
    And ere three howres to ende were fully
tryde,
Home came she first; welcome, (quoth I), and well
    hyde.
Yea, *a short horse is soone currid*, (quoth shee);
But *the weaker hath the woorse* we all may see.
And after our last parting, my husband and I
Departed, each to place agreed formerly.
Myne uncle and aunt on me did loure and glome,
Both bad me good speed, but none bad me welcome.
Their folkes glomd on me too, by which it appeareth,
The yong cocke croweth as he the old heareth.
At dinner they were, and made, (for manners' sake),
A kinswoman of ours me to table take;
A false flattring filth, and if that be good,
None better *to beare two faces in one hood.*[3]

---

[3] *To beare two faces in one hood.*

Alberto. Not play two parts in one? away, away, 'tis common
fashion. Nay, if you cannot bear two subtle fronts under one
hood; ideot, goe by, goe by; off this world's stage! O times im-
puritie!—*Antonio and Mellida,* 1602.

She speaketh as shee would creepe into your bosome.

And when the meale mouth hath woon the bottome

Of your stomacke, then will the pickthanke[4] it tell

To your most enimies you to buy and sell.

To tell tales out of schoole, that is her great lust.

Looke what shee knowth, *blab it wist and out it must.*[5]

There is no moe such titifyls in Englandes ground,

To hold with the hare and run with the hound.

Fyre in the tone hand and water in the tother,

The makebate beareth betweene brother and brother.

She can winke on the yew and werye the lam ;

She maketh earnest matters of every flimflam ;

Shel'e *have an ore in every man's barge ;*[6]

And no man may chat ought in ought of her charge.

Coll under candlestick[7] shee can play on both handes ;

---

[4] *Pickthanke* is an opprobrious term to denote a person who tries to place people under small obligations by performing trivial services. In *Henry IV.*, Pt. 1. iii. 2, "smiling pickthanks and base news mongers."

[5] *Blab it wist and out it must.*

> Labbe hyt whyste
> and owt yt muste.

MS. Harleian, circa 1490.

[6] *Have an ore in every man's barge.*

Somewhat earlier, the proverb is found in a ballad entitled "Long have I bene a singing man," by John Redford, circa 1540.

[7] *Coll under candlestick.*

There was a Christmas game so called. The meaning of "coll" is to embrace, to kiss.

Dissimulation well she understandes.

She is *lost with an apple and woon with a nut;*[8]

Her *toung is no edge-toole but yet it will cut.*

But *little titte all tayle;* I have heard ere this,

As high as two horse loves[9] her person is.

For privy nips or castes overthwart[10] the shinnes,

Hee shall leese the maistry that with her beginnes.

Shee is, to turne love to hate, or joy to greefe,

A paterne *as meete as a rope for a theefe.*

Her promise of friendship for any availe,

Is *as sure to hold as an ele by the tayle.*

Shee is *nether fish, nor flesh, nor good red herring.*[11]

Shee is a ringleader there.   And I fearing

---

[8] *Lost with an apple and woon with a nut.*

Exactly similar to this is the proverb occurring in GASCOIGNE'S *Ferdinando* :— .

> Nor woman true, but even as stories tell
> Wonne with an egge and lost againe with shell.

[9] *As high as two horse loves.*

It was formerly not unusual to feed horses on loaves of bread, composed of wheat and beans.   These loaves became jocularly a standard of measurement.

Her stature scant three horse loaves did exceed.—HARRING-TON'S *Ariosto.*

[10] *Overthwart.*

It is singular that the word "overthwart," though common with his contemporaries, is not once used by Shakespeare.

[11] *Nether fish, nor flesh, nor good red herring.*

I have discovered no earlier instance of the use of this proverb, though a simpler form is frequently to be met with, as :—

She would spit her venim, thought it not evil
To set up a candle before the devill.[12]
I clawd her by the backe in way of a charme,
To do me, not the more good, but the lesse harme ;
Praying her, in her eare, on my syde to houlde ;
Shee thereto swearing by her false fayth, she would.
Streight after dinner myne aunt had no choice,
But other burst, or burst out *in Pilat's voice.*
Yee huswife, what wind blowth ye hyther this night ?
Yee might have knockt ere ye came in, *leave is light.*
Better unborne then untaught,[13] I have heard say ;
But ye be *better fed then taught* farre away.
Not very fat fed, sayd this flebergebet ;[14]

Prince Henry. An otter, sir John ! why an otter?
Falstaff. Why? she is neither fish nor flesh ; a man knows not
where to have her.

Later the proverb occurs in DRYDEN, *Epilogue to the Duke of Guise* :—

> Damned neuters in their middle way of steering,
> Are neither fish nor flesh nor good red herring.

[12] *To set up a candle before the devill.*

Roger. Troth Mistresse, what doe I looke like now ?
Bellafronte. Like as you are : a panderly, sixpenny rascall.
Roger. I may thanke you for that : in faith I looke like an old
Proverbe, Hold the candle before the devill.—DECKER'S *Honest
W——*, 1604.

[13] *Better unborne then untaught.*

Old men yn proverbe sayde by old tyme, ' A chyld were beter to
be unbore, Than to be untaught.'—SYMON'S *Lessons of Wysedome
for all Maner Chyldryn*, circa 1450.

[14] *Flebergebet.*

Fratteretto, Fleberdigebet, Hoberdidanæ, Torobatto, were four

But *neede hath no law;* need maketh her hither jet.

She comth, neece Ales, (quoth she), for that is her name,

More for neede than for kyndnes, peine of shame.

Howbeit she cannot lacke, for *he fyndeth that seekes;*

Lovers live by love as Larkes live by leekes;

Sayd this Ales, much more than halfe in mockage.

Tush, (quoth myne aunt), these lovers in dotage

Thinke the ground beare them not, but wed of corage

They must in all hast; though a leafe of borage

Might buye all the substance that they can sell.

Well aunt, (quoth Ales), *all is well that endes well.*

Yea, Ales, *of a good beginning comth a good end.*[15]

Not so good to borow, as be able to lend.

Nay indeed aunt, (quoth she), it is sure so ;

She must needes graunt she hath wrought her own woe.

She thought, Ales, shee had *seene far in a milstone,*[16]

---

devils of the round or morice ; these four had forty assistants under them, as themselves do confesse.—HARSENET'S *Declaration of Popish Impostures.*

[15] *Of a good beginning comth a good end.*

> But in proverbe I have herde saie,
> That who that well his warke beginneth,
> The rather a good ende he winneth.
> > GOWER, *Confessio Amantis.*

[16] *Seene far in a milstone.*

Another illustration of the early use of this proverbial saying may be culled from LYLY'S *Euphues and his England.*

Then Fidus, your eies are so sharp that you cannot onely looke through a milstone, but cleane through the minde, and so cunning that you can levell at the dispositions of women you never knew.

When she got a husband, and namely such one,
As they by wedding could not onely nought win,
But lose both living and love of all their kin.
Good aunt, (quoth I), humbly I beseech yee,
My trespasse done unto you forgive it me.
I know and knowledge I have wrought mine own payne,
But thinges past my handes, I can not call agayne.
True, (quoth Ales), *thinges done cannot be undone,*
Be they done in due tyme, too late or too soone :
But *better late then never*[17] to repent this.
Too late, (quoth myne aunt), this repentaunce shewd
        is;
When the steede is stolne shut the stable durre.[18]
I tooke her for a rose, but she breedeth a burre.

---

[17] *Better late then never.*
Again in TUSSER'S *Five Hundred Points of Good Husbandry.*

[18] *When the steede is stolne shut the stable durre.*

> Quant fol par noun saver
> Ad perdu soun aver,
> E il est ben matez
> E 'eus garder nel saver
> Mès si ore le avei
> Touz tens averei asez
> Quant le cheval est emblé dounke ferme fols l'estable.
> Ces dist le vilain.
>   *Les Proverbes del Vilain,* circa 1300.

The steede was stollen before I shut the gate,
The cates consumed before I smelt the feast.
                         Devises of Sundrie Gentlemen.

Shee comth to sticke to me now in her lacke,

Rather to rent off my clothes from my backe,

Than to doe me one farthing woorth of good.

I see day at this litle hole. For *this bood*

Shewth what fruite will follow. In good faith,'I sayd,

In way of your petition I sue for your ayd.

A well, (quoth she), now I well understand,

The walking staffe hath caught warmth in your hand.

A cleane fingred huswife, and an idle, folke say,

And will be lyme-fingred, I feare by my faye.

It is *as tender as a Parsons lemman ;*

Nought can shee dooe, and what can shee have than ?

As sober as shee seemeth fewe dayes come about,

But shee will once *wash her face in an ale clout ;*

And then betweene her and the rest of the rout,

I proud, and thou proud, who shall beare th'ashes out.

She may not beare a feather, but shee must breath,

She maketh so much of her paynted sheath.

She thinkes her farthing good silver,[19] I tell you,

But *for a farthing who ever did sell you,*

Might bost you to be better solde than bought.

And yet though she be worth nought, nor have nought,

---

[19] *She thinkes her farthing good silver.*

Pandarina. Take example at me ; I tell you I thought my half-peny good silver within these few yeares past, and no man esteem-eth me unlesse it be for counsell.—GASCOIGNE'S *Glasse of Govern-ment,* 1575.

Her gowne is gayer and better then myne.

At her gaye gowne, (quoth Ales), ye may repine,

How be it as we may, we love to goe gay all.

Well, well, (quoth myne aunt), *pryde will have a fall;*

For pryde goeth before and shame commeth after.[20]

Sure, (sayd Ales), in manner of mocking laughter,

There is nothing in this world that agreeth wurse,

Then doth a Ladies hart and a beggers purse.

But pryde she sheweth none, her looke reason alloweth,

She lookth as butter would not melt in her mouth.[21]

Well, *the still sow eats up all the draffe,*[1] Ales.

---

[20] *Pryde goeth before, &c.*

    Pryde gothe before and shame cometh behynde :
    Alas that Englyshe men sholde be so blynde,
    So moche sorowe amonge us and so lytell fere
    We may wayle the tyme that ever it came here.

                Treatise of a Gallant, circa 1510.

[21] *She lookth as butter would not melt in her mouth.*

A cette parolle mist dame Mehault ses mains à ses costez et en grant couroux luy respondy que. . . . et que, Dieu merci, aincores fondoit le burre en sa bouche, combien qu'elle ne peust croquier noisettes, car elle n'avoit que un seul dent.—*Les Evangiles des Quenouilles*, circa 1475.

[1] *The still sow eats up all the draffe.*

A "still sow" was a term of reproach for a sly lurking fellow ; "draff" is anything unfit for human food.

Mrs. Page. Wives may be merry, and yet honest too :
We do not act, that often jest and laugh ;
'Tis old but true, stil swine eat all the draff.

                Merry Wives of Windsor, iv. 2.

All is not gold that glisters,[2] by told tales.

In youth she was toward and without evill ;

But *soone ripe, soone rotten ;*[3] *yong saint, old devill.*[4]

How be it, lo *God sendth the shrewd cowe short hornes.*[5]

While she was in this house *she sate upon thornes,*

Each on day was three, till liberty was borow,

For one months joy to bring her whole lyves sorow.

It were pitty, (quoth Ales), but she should do well ;

For beauty and stature *she beareth the bell.*[6]

---

[2] *All is not gold that glisters.*

> Uns proverbes dit et raconte
> Que tout n'est pas ors c'on voit luire.
>> *Li Diz de freire Denise cordelier,* circa 1300.

All things that shineth is not by and by pure gold.—*Ralph Roister Doister,* 1566.

Is found in CHAUCER'S *Chanones Yemannes Tale,* and in LYDGATE'S poem *On the Mutability of Human Affairs.*

[3] *Soone ripe, soone rotten.*

Occurs in HARMAN'S *Caveat for Common Cursitors,* 1567.

[4] *Yong saint, old devill.*

Young seynt, old devyl.—*MS. Harleian,* circa 1490.

[5] *God sendth the shrewd cowe short hornes.*

The Bishop of Sarum sayd, That he trusted ere Christmas Day to visit and cleanse a good part of the kingdom. But most commonly God sendeth a shrewd cow short horns, or else many a thousand in England had smarted.—FOXE, *Acts and Monuments.*

[6] *She beareth the bell.*

In horse-racing, a bell was formerly the prize competed for, hence the epitaph :—

> Here lyes the man whose horse did gaine
> The bell, in race on Salisbury plain.

Ill weede growth fast,[1] Ales : whereby the corne is lorne ;
For surely the weede overgroweth the corne.
Yee prayse the wine before yee taste of the grape ;
But she can no more harme than can a shee ape.
It is a good body, her property preeves :
Shee lacketh but even a new pare of sleeves.
If I may, (as they say), tell troth without sinne,
Of troth she is *a wolfe in a lambes skinne.*
Her hart is ful hie, when her eie is ful low ;
A guest as good lost as found, for all this show ;
But *many a good cow hath an evill caulfe.*
I speake this daughter in thy mother's behalfe,
My sister, (God rest her soule), whom though I bost,
Was cald the floure of honesty in this cost.
Aunt, (quoth I), I take for father and mother,
Myne uncle and you above all other.
When we would, ye would not be our child, (quoth she) ;
Wherefore now whan yee would, now will not wee.

---

[1] *Ill weede growth fast.*
Mother.   Good Lord !
      How you have grown ! Is he not Alexander ?
Alex. Yes, truly, he's shot up finely, God be thanked !
Mercury. An ill weed, mother, will do so.
Alex. You say true, sir, an ill weed grows apace
              BEAUMONT AND FLETCHER, *The Coxcomb.*

      Ewyl weed ys sone y-growe.
                    MS. Harleian, circa 1490.

Since thou wouldst needes cast away thy selfe thus,

Thou shalt sure sinke in thyne owne sinne for us.

Aunt, (quoth I), after a doting or drunken deede,

Let submission obtayne some mercy or meede.

Hee that kilth a man when he is drunke, (quoth she),

Shal be hangd when he is sober. And he

Whom in itching no scratching will forbeare,

He must beare the smarting that shall follow there.

And thou being borne very nigh of my stocke,

Though nye be my kirtell, yet neere is my smocke.[8]

I have one of myne owne whome I must looke to.

Yea aunt, (quoth Ales), that thing must ye needes doe ;

Nature compelth you to set your own first up ;

For I have heard say, *it is a deere collup*[9]

That is cut out of th' owne flesh. But yet aunt,

So small may her request be, that ye may grant

To satisfy the same, which may do her good,

And you no harme, in avauncing of your owne blood.

---

[8] *Though nye be my kirtell, &c.*

Beside, there is a antiquitie a proverb no lesse practised then common, which is, Nearer unto mee is my shirt then my coate ; by following of which, every man commonly loveth his owne profit more then others.—*The Contention betweene three Brethren; the Whore-monger, the Drunkard, and the Dice Player*, 1608.

[9] *Collup.*

God knows thou art a colup of my flesh.

1 *Henry VI.* v. 5.

E

And cosin, (quoth she to me), what ye would crave,
Declare, that our aunt may know what ye would have ?
Nay, (quoth I), be the winners all loosers,
Folke say alway, *beggers should be no choosers.* [10]
With thanks I shal take what ever myne aunt please;
Where nothing is, a little thing doth ease ;
Hunger maketh hard beans sweet.   Where saddles lack,
Better ryde on a pad than on the horse bare backe.
And by this proverbe appeareth this one thing,
That alway *somewhat is better then nothing.*
Hold fast whan ye have it, (quoth she) ; by my lyfe,
The boy thy husband, and thou the girle, his wife,
Shall not consume that I have labored fore.
Thou art yong ynough, and I can worke no more.
Kyt Calot, [11] my cosin, saw this thus farre on,

---

[10] *Beggers should be no choosers.*

Loveless. What dost thou mean to do with thy children, Savil ?
Savil. My eldest boy is half a rogue already ;
He was born bursten ; and your worship knows,
That is a pretty step to men's companions.
My youngest boy I purpose, sir, to bind
For ten years to a gaoler, to draw under him,
That he may shew us mercy in his function,
        *   *   *   *   *
Beggers must be no choosers ;
In every place, I take it, but the stocks.
        BEAUMONT AND FLETCHER, *Scornful Lady,* v. 3.

[11] *Kyt Calot.*

Kit Callot and Giles Hather are said to have been the first

And in myne auntes eare she whispreth anon,

Roundly these wordes, to make this matter whole,—

Aunt, *let them that be a colde blow at the cole.*[12]

They shall for me, Ales, (quoth she), by God's blist.

She and I have shaken handes.   Farewell unkist.

And thus with a beck as good as a *dieu-gard*,

She flang fro me, and I from her hitherward.

Begging of her booteth *not the woorth of a beane ;*

Little knoweth the fat sow what the leane doth meane.

Forsooth, (quoth I), ye have bestird ye well ;

But where was your uncle while all this fray fell ?

Asleepe by, (quoth she), routing lyke a hogge ;

And *it is evill waking of a sleeping dogge.*

The bitch and her whelpe might have bene a sleepe
    too,

For ought they in waking to me would doo.

Fare ye well, (quoth she).   I will now home streight,

And at my husbandes handes for better newes weight.

English persons who took up the occupation of gipsies.   Hence
the use of the word 'calot' as a term of abuse.   It is variously
spelt and is used generally to denote a scold or infamous woman.

  Gogs bread ! and thinkes the callet thus to keep the neele me
fro.—*Gammer Gurtons Needle,* 1560.

  [12] *Let them that be a colde blow at the cole.*

> Our talwod is all brent,
> Our fagottes are all spent,
> We may blow at the cole.

Why come ye not to Court, by JOHN SKELTON, circa 1520.

CHAPTER XI.

E that came to me the next day before noone :
What tydinges now, (quoth I), how have ye
doone ?
Upon our departing, (quoth he), yesterday,
Toward myne uncle's, somewhat more than midway,
I overtooke a man, a servant of his,
And a frend of myne.   Who gessed streight with this
What myne errand was, offring in the same
To doe his best for me ; and so in God's name
Thither we went ; no body being within,
But myne uncle, myne aunt, and one of our kin,
A made knave, as it were a rayling gester,
Not a more gaggling gander hence to Chester.
At sight of me he asked, who have we there ?
I have seene this gentleman, if I wist where ;
How be it, lo, *seldom seene, soone forgotten.*
He was, (as he will be), some what cupshotten.
Six dayes in the weeke, beside the market day,
Malt is above wheat with him, market men say.
But for as much as I saw the same taunt,
Contented well mine uncle and myne aunt,

And that I came to fall in and not to fall out,

I forbare, or else his drunken red snout

I would have made as oft to chaunge from hew to
      hew,

As doth cockes of Inde.   For this is true,

It is a small hop on the thombe.[13]   And Christ wot,

It is wood at a woord ; *litle pot soone hot.*[14]

Now *mery as a cricket,* and by and by,

Angry as a waspe, though in both no cause why.

But he was at home there, he might speake his will,

Every cocke is proud on his owne dunghill.[15]

I shall be even with him herein when I can.

But he having done, thus myne uncle began,—

Ye marchant what attempth you to attempt us,

To come on us before the messenger thus ?

---

[13] *Hop on the thombe.*

A term of contempt applied to diminutive persons.

Plain friend hop o' my thumb, know you who we are ?—*Taming of the Shrew.*

[14] *Little pot soone hot.*

Now were I not a little pot, and soon hot, my very lips might freeze to my very teeth, ... for, considering the weather, a taller man than I will take cold.—*Taming of the Shrew,* iv. 1.

[15] *Every cocke is proude on his owne dunghill.*

þet fleshs is her et home, ase eorðe, þet is et eorðe : aut for þui hit is cwointe ᵗ cwiuer, °ase me seið, " þet coc is kene on his owne mixenne."—*þe Ancren Riwle,* circa 1250.

Roming in and out, I here tell how ye tosse,

But sonne, *the rolling stone never gatherth mossc.*[16]

Lyke a pickpurse pilgrim ye prie and ye proule

At rovers, *to robbe Peter and pay Poule.*[17]

I wis I know ere any more be tolde,

That *draffe is your errand, but drinke ye wold.*[18]

Uncle, (quoth I), of the cause for which I come,

I pray you patiently heare the whole summe.

In fayth, (quoth hee), without any more summing,

---

[16] *The rolling stone never gatherth mosse.*

Herod. Speake thou three-legd tripos, is thy shippe of fooles a flote yet?

Dondolo. I ha many things in my head to tell you.

Herod. I, thy head is alwaies working; it roles, and it roles, Dondolo, but it gathers no mosse, Dondolo.—*The Fawn,* 1606, by JOHN MARSTON.

Pierre volage ne queult mousse.—*De l'hermite qui se désespéra pour le larron qui ala en paradis avant que lui,* 13th century.

[17] *To robbe Peter and pay Poule.*

The proverb is said to have derived its origin when, in the reign of Edward VI., the lands of St. Peter at Westminster were appropriated to raise money for the repair of St. Paul's in London. It must be recollected that the first edition of Heywood's book appeared at the precise time that this arrangement was either being determined upon or being executed. The French form of the proverb, " découvrir saint Pierre pour couvrir saint Paul" gives additional colouring to the statement.

[18] *Draffe is your errand, but drinke ye wold.*

Again in LYLY'S *Euphues,* 1579.

I know to beg of me is thy comming.

Forsoth, (quoth his man), it is so indeede ;

And I dare boldly boste, if yee knew his neede,

Yee would of pitty yet set him in some stay.

Sonne, *better be envied than pitied*, folke say :

And for his cause of pitye, (had hee had grace),

Hee might this day have bene cleere out of the case,

But now hee hath *well fisht and caught a frogge ;* [19]

Where nought is to wed with, wise men flee the clog. [20]

Where I, (quoth I), did not as yee will or bad,

That repent I oft, and as oft wish I had.

Sonne, (quoth he), as I have heard of myne olders,

---

[19] *Well fisht and caught a frogge.*

So again writes LATIMER in his *Remaines :*—

> Well I have fished and caught a frog,
> Brought little to pass with much ado.

[20] "*A clog,*" from originally meaning an incumbrance, came in process of time to mean a wife. In its latter sense we find its use as well as its definition in a very early literary remnant :—

> *Science.* Ye have woon me for ever dowghter.
> Although ye have woon a clogg wyth all.
> *Wyt.* A clogg, sweete hart, what?
> *Science.* Such as doth fall
> To all men that joyne themselves in marriage.
> > *Play of Wyt and Science,* circa 1540.

Again in *Winter's Tale,* iv. 4 :—

> The prince himself is about a piece of iniquity,
> Stealing away from his father with his clog at his heels.

Wishers and wolders bee no good housholders ;[1]
This proverbe for a lesson, with such other.
Not lyke, (as who sath), the sonne of my brother,
But lyke myne owne sonne, I oft before told thee
To cast her quite of, but it would not hold thee.
Whan I wild thee any other whether to goe,
Tush, there was no *moe maydes but Malkin*[2] thoe !
Yee had been lost, to lacke your lust when yee list,
By two myles trudging twise a weeke to bee kist.
I would yee had kist, well I will no more sturre ;
It is good to have a hatch before the durre.[3]

---

[1] *Wishers and wolders bee no good housholders.*

The earliest occurrence of this proverb is probably that in
Vulgaria Stambrigi, printed circa 1510 :—

Wysshers and wolders ben smal housholders.

Francisco was set at libertie and hee and Isabel, joyntly together taking themselves to a little cottage, began to be as Cicero-
nicall as they were amorous . . . . for he being a scholer, and
nurst up at the universities, resolved rather to live by his wit, then
any way to be pinched with want, thinking this old sentence to
be true, the wishers and woulders were never good house-holders.
—GREEN'S *Never too Late*, 1590.

[2] *Moe maydes but Malkin.*

" Malkin," a form of Mary, was used to denote a slattern, and
in many parts of England is still the name for a scarecrow.

The kitchen malkin pins
Her richest lockram 'bout her reechy neck.
Coriolanus, ii. 1.

[3] *It is good to have a hatch before the durre.*

A hatch is a wooden partition coming over the lower half of a

But *who will in tyme present pleasure refrayne,*
Shall in time to come the more pleasure obtayne.
Follow pleasure, and then will pleasure flee ;
Flee pleasure, and pleasure will follow thee.
And how is my saying come to passe now ?
How oft did I prophecie this betweene you
And your Ginifinee Nycebecetur,
Whan sweete sugre should turne to soure salt petur ?
Whereby yee should in seeing that yee never saw,
Thinke that you never thought, your selfe a daw.[4]

---

doorway and leaving open the upper half. In the time of Queen Elizabeth, disreputable houses were distinguished by hatches surmounted with iron spikes. To frequent places of that description was politely called " to go the manor of pickt hatch "; and the nickname Pickt Hatch was bestowed on certain parts of Elizabethan London in the neighbourhood of Turnmill Street, Clerkenwell. So we find in *Merry Wives of Windsor,*—

To your manor of pickt hatch go !

[4] *A daw, i.e.,* a foolish fellow.

Humphrey Dixon said of Nicholas Brestney, utter Barrester and Counsellor of Gray's-Inn. Thou a Barrester? Thou art no Barrester, thou art a Barretor ; thou wert put from the Bar, and thou darest not shew thyself there. Thou study Law? Thou hast as much wit as a Daw. Upon not guilty pleaded, the Jury found for the plaintiff, and assessed damages to £23, upon which judgment was given: and in a Writ of Error in the Exchequer Chamber, the judgment was affirmed.—*Coke's Reports.*

Good faith, I am no wiser than a daw.
1 Henry VI. ii. 4.

An earlier instance of this application of the word is found in *The Four Elements,* circa 1510 :—

But that tyme yee thought me a daw, so that I
Did no good in al my wordes then, save onely
Approved this proverbe plaine and true matter ;
A man may well bring a horse to the water,
But he cannot make him drinke without he will.
Colts, (quoth his man), may prove well with tatches ill,
For *of a ragged colt there comth a good horse.*[5]
If he be good now, of his ill past no force.
Well, he that hangeth himselfe on Sunday, (said he),
Shall hang still uncut downe on Monday for me.
I have hangd up my hatchet, God speed him well.
A wonder thing what things these old things tell.
Cat after kinde good mouse hunt. And also
Men say, *kinde will creepe where it may not goe.*[6]
Commonly all things shewth from whence it camme ;
The litter is like to the sire and the damme ;

He that for commyn welth bysyly
   Studyeth and laboryth, and lyveth by Goddes law
   Except he waxe ryche, men count hym but a daw !

[5] *Of a ragged colt, &c.*

Touchstone. This cannot be fained, sure. Heaven pardon my severitie ! "The ragged colt may prove a good horse."—*Eastward Hoe,* 1605.

[6] *Kinde will creepe where it may not goe.*

Thurio. How now, sir Proteus ? are you crept before us ?
Proteus. Ay, gentle Thurio ; for you know that love
Will creep in service when it cannot go.

Two Gentlemen of Verona, iv. 2.

How can the foale amble if the horse and mare trot?
These sentences are assigned unto thy lot,
By conditions of thy father and mother,
My sister in law, and mine owne said brother.
Thou followest their steps *as right as a line.*
For when provander prickt them a little time,
They did as thy wife and thou did, both dote
Each on other; and being not worth a grote,
Then went (witlesse) to wedding.   Whereby at last
They both went a begging.   And even the like cast
Hast thou ; *thou wilt beg or steale ere thou die.*
Take heed, friend, I have seene *as far come as nie.*
If ye seeke *to finde things ere they be lost,*
Ye shall find one day ye come to your cost.
This doe I but repeate, for this I tolde thee ;
And more I say, but I could not then hold thee ;
Nor will not hold thee now ; nor such follie feele,
To set at my heart that thou settest at thy heele.
And as of my good ere I one grote give,
I will see how my wife and my selfe may live.
Thou goest a gleaning ere the cart have carried,
But ere thou gleane ought, since thou wouldst be married.
Shall I make thee laugh now, and my selfe weepe then ?
Nay good childe, *better children weepe then old men.*[7]

---

[7] *Better children weepe then old men.*
These words are memorable from a well-known episode in the

Men should not prease much to spend much upon fooles ;
Fish is cast away that is cast in drie pooles.
To flee charge, and finde ease, ye would now here oste ;
It is easie *to crie ble*[8] at other mens cost ;
But *a bow long bent, at length must ware weake.*
Long bent I toward you, but that bent I will breake.
Fare well, and feede full, that love ye well to doo,
But you lust not to doe that longeth theretoo.
The cat would eate fish and would not wet her feete.[9]
They must hunger in frost that will not worke in heete.
And *he that will thrive must aske leave of his wife ;*[10]
But your wife will give none ; by your and her life,

Gowrie conspiracy. King James VI. about to depart fron Gowrie
Castle was forcibly prevented by the Master of Glammis, and as
the tears started to the eyes of the young king, " better bairns
weep than bearded men" is recorded to have been the other's
observation.

[8] *To cry ble.*

One of the *Hundred Mery Tales*, circa 1525, is entitled " Of
the husbande that cryed ble under the bed."

[9] *The cat would eate fish and would not wet her feete.*

Shakespeare thus alludes to this proverb in *Macbeth :—*

> Letting, I dare not, wait upon, I would,
> Like the poor cat i' the adage.

> Cat lufat visch, ac he nele his feth wete.
>   *MS. Trin. Coll. Camb.,* circa 1250.

[10] *He that will thrive, &c.*

Another proverb rather more vaguely lays down the conditions
of prosperity :—

It is hard to wive and thrive both in a yeare.[11]
Thus by wiving, thy thriving doth so appeare,
That thou art past thrift before thrift begin.
But loe, *will will have will,* though will woe win.
Will is a good sonne and will is a shrewd boy :
And wilfull shrewd will hath wrought thee this toy,
A gentle white spurre, and at neede a sure speare ;
He standeth now as he had *a flea in the eare.*
How be it for any great curtesie he doth make,
It seemeth the gentleman *hath eaten a stake.*
He beareth a dagger in his sleeve, trust me,
To kill all that he meeteth prouder then he.
He will perke, I heare say he must have the bench ;
Jacke would be a gentleman if he could speake French.[12]

He had a sonne or twaine he would advaunce,
And sayd they should take paines untyll it fell ;
He that wyll thrive (quod he) must tary chaunce.
—*Debate betweene Pride and Lowliness,* by FRANCIS THYNN,
1570.

[11] *It is hard to wive and thrive both in a yeare.*
  Primus Pastor. It is sayde full ryfe,
    A man may not wyfe
    And also thryfe
    And alle in a yere.
                    Townely Mysteries, circa 1420.

[12] *Jacke would be a gentleman if he could speake French.*
The proverb is obviously a relic of the Norman subver-
sion of England. Speaking of the rule of the Anglo-Norman

He thinketh his feete be where his head shall never
 come.

He would faine flee, but he wanteth fethers, some.

Sir, (quoth his man), he will no fault defend ;

But hard is for any man all faults to mend ;

He is liveles, that is faultles, old folkes thought.

He hath, (quoth he), *but one fault, he is starke nought.*

Well, (quoth his man), *the best cart may overthrow.*

Carts well driven, (quoth he), goe long upright thow.

But for my reward, let him no longer tarier ;

I will send it him by Jong Long the carier.

O helpe him sir, (said he), since yee easily may.

Shamefull craving, (quoth he), *must have shamefull nay.*

Yee may sir, (quoth he), *mend three nayes with one yee.*

Two false knaves neede no broker,[13] men say, (sayd hee).

---

kings, the elder Disraeli writes :—" This was the time when it
was held a shame among Englishmen to appear English. It
became proverbial to describe a Saxon who ambitioned some
distinguished rank, that " he would be a gentleman if he could
but talk French."—*Amenities of Literature.*

[13] *Two false knaves neede no broker.*

   Some will say,
  A crafty knave need no broker,
  But here's a craftie knave and a broker too.
    A Knacke to Knowe a Knave, 1594.

As two false knaves need no Broker, for they can easily
enough agree in wickednesse *fine mediante,* without any to
breake the matter betweene them: so among true and faithfull
men, there need no others.—*A Sword against Swearers,* 1611.

Some say also, *it is merry when knaves meete.*[14]

But *the moe knaves, the woorse company to greete;*

The one knave now croucheth, while thother cravith.

But to shew what shall be his relevavith,

Either after my death, if my will bee kept,

Or during my lyfe : had I this hall hept

With gold, he may his part on good Fryday eate,

And fast never the woorse for ought hee shall get.

These former lessons cond, take foorth this, sonne.

Tell thy cards, and then tell me what thou hast won?

Now here is the dore and there is the way :

And so, (quoth hee), farewell gentle Geffray.

Thus parted I from him, being much dismayde,

A "broker" formerly meant any medium or go-between, hence also something discreditable.

Madam, I am no broker !

BEAUMONT AND FLETCHER, *Valentin*, ii. 2.

[14] *It is merry when knaves meete.*

No more of Cocke now I wryte,

But mery it is when knaves done mete.

Cocke Lorelles Bote, circa 1510.

Gentleman. But where's the new Booke thou telst me of ?

Prentice. Mary, looke you, sir : this is a prettie meeting here in London betweene a Wife, a Widow, and a Mayde.

Gentleman. Merrie meeting ? why that Title is stale. There's a Boke cald Tis merry when knaves meete, and there's a Ballad Tis merry when Malt-men meete ; and besides there's an old Proverbe The more the merrier.—*Tis Merrie when Gossips meete*, by SAMUEL ROWLANDS, 1602.

Which his man saw, and to comfort mee, sayd :

What man, plucke up your harte, bee of good cheere !

After cloudes blacke, wee shall have wether cleere.

What should your face thus againe the wool be shorne

For one fall ? What man *all this wind shakes no corne !*

Let this wind overblow ; a tyme I will spye,

To take winde and tyde with mee and speed thereby.

I thanke you, (quoth I), but *great boste and small roste*

Maketh unsavery mouthes, where ever men oste.

And this bost very unsavorly serveth,

For *while the grasse groweth the horse starveth.*[15]

Better one byrde in hand than ten in the wood.[16]

Rome was not built in one day (quoth he),[17] and yet stood

---

[15] *While the grasse groweth, &c.*

Whylst grass doth growe, oft sterves the seely steede.
            WHETSTONE'S *Promos and Cassandra*, 1578.

   Hamlet. Ay, sir, but, While the grass grows,—
The proverb is something musty.
                    Hamlet, iii. 2.

[16] *Better one byrde in hand, &c.*

An old proverbe makyth with thys whyche I tak good.
Better one byrd in hand then ten in the wood.
        HEYWOOD'S *Dialogue on Wit and Folly*, circa 1530.

[17] *Rome was not built in one day.*

Hæc tamen vulgaris sententia me aliquantulum recreavit, quæ
etsi non auferre, tamen minuere possit dolorem meum, quæ quidem
sententia hæc est, Romam uno die non fuisse conditam.—*Extem-
pore speech by Queen Elizabeth before the University of Cambridge*, 9th August, 1564.

Till it was finisht, as some say, full fayre.

Your heart is in your hose[18] all in dispayre.

But as every man sayeth *a dog hath a day,*

Should a man dispayre than any day ? nay.

Yee have many strings to your bowe,[19] for yee know,

Though I, having the bent of your uncles bow,

Can no way bring your bolt in the butte to stand ;

Yet have yee other markes to rove at hand.

The kayes hang not all by one man's girdle, man.

Though nought will be woon here, I say, yet yee can

Taste other kinsmen, of whom yee may get

Here some and there some, *many small make a great.*[20]

---

[18] *Your heart is in your hose.*

Primus Pastor. Breck outt youre voce, let se as ye yelp.
Tercius Pastor. I may not for the pose bot I have help.
Secundus Pastor. A, thy hert is in thy hose.
                                Towneley Mysteries, circa 1430.

[19] *Yee have many strings to your bowe.*

I am wel pleased to take any coulor to defend your honor, and hope that you wyl remember, that who seaketh two stringes to one bowe, the may shute strong, but never strait ; and if you suppose that princes causes be vailed so covertly that no intelligence can bewraye them, deceave not your-selfe ; we old foxes can find shiftes to save ourselves by others malice and come by knowledge of greattest secreat, spetiallye if it touche our freholde. —*Letter of Queen Elizabeth to James VI.,* June, 1585.

[20] *Many small make a great.*

The proverbe saith that many a small makith a grete.— CHAUCER, *Persons Tale.*

F

For come light winnings with blessings or curses,
Evermore *light gaynes make heavie purses.*
Children learne to creepe ere they can learne to goe ;
By little and little yee must learne even so.
Throw no gift againe at the givers head ;
For *better is halfe a lofe than no bread.*
I may begge my bread, (quoth I), for my kin all
That dwelth nye.　Well yet, (quoth he), and the worst
　　.fall,
Yee may to your kinsman, hence nine or ten myle,
Rich without charge, whom yee saw not of long while.
That benchwhistler, (quoth I), is a pinchpeny,
As free of gift as a poore man of his eye.
He is *hie in th' instep, and so streight laste,*
That pride and covetyse withdraweth all repaste.
Yee know what he hath been, (quoth he), but ywis,
Absence sayth plainely, ye know not what he is.
Men know, (quoth I), I have heard now and then,
How the market goeth by the market men.
Further it is said, who that saying wayeth,
It must needs be true that every man sayeth.
Men say also, *children and fooles cannot lye ;*[1]

---

[1] *Children and fooles cannot lye.*

Master Constable says : " You know neighbours 'tis an old saw,
Children and fooles speake true."—LYLY'S *Endimion*, 1591.

And both man and childe sayth, he is a hensby.
And myselfe knowth him, I dare boldly brag,
Even *as well as the begger knowth his bag.*[2]
And I knew him not worth a gray grote ;
He was at an ebbe, though he be now a flote.
Poore as the poorest.   And now nought he setteth
By poore folke.   For *the parish priest forgetteth
That ever he hath been holy water Clarke.*
By ought I can now heare, or ever could marke,
Of no man hath he pitie or compassion.
Well, (quoth he), every man after his fashion.
He may yet pitie you, for ought doth appeare :
It hapth in one houre that hapth not in seven yeare.
Forspeake not your fortune, nor hide not your neede ;
*Nought venter nought have; spare to speak, spare to speed;
Unknowne, unkist ; it is lost that is unsought.*
As good seeke nought, (quoth I), *as seeke and finde nought.*
It is, (quoth I), *ill fishing before the net.*
But though we get little, *deare bought and far fet
Are dainties for Ladies.*[3]   Goe we both two ;

---

[2] *As well as the begger knowth his bag.*

As well as the begger knows his dish, is another form of this
proverb found in *The Burning of Paules Church in London, by*
Bishop Pilkington, 1561.

[3] *Deare bought and far fet are dainties for Ladies.*

Niece. Ay, marry, sir, this was a rich conceit indeed.

I have for my master thereby to doo.

I may breake a dish there.   And sure I shall

Set all at sixe and seven,[4] to win some windfall.

And I will *hang the bell about the cat's necke ;*[5]

For I will first breake and jeoperd the first checke.

Pompey. And far fetched ; therefore good for you, lady.
>   BEAUMONT and FLETCHER, *Wit at several*
>   *Weapons.*

Some far fet trick, good for ladies, some stale toy or other.
>   MARSTON'S *Malcontent.*

[4] *Set all at sixe and seven.*

In the *Towneley Mysteries* the Deity is described as He that
" set alle on seven," that is, set or appointed everything in seven
days.   To set at six and seven, or more modernly, "to be at
sixes and sevens," Mr. Halliwell supposes to be the reverse of
this, to disarrange, to put into disorder.

Herod, in his anger at the Wise Men, exclaims :—

>   Bot be thay past me by, by Mahowne in heven,
>   I shalle, and that in hy, set alle on sex and seven.
>   *Towneley Mysteries,* circa 1420.

>   All is uneven,
>   And everything is left at six and seven.
>   *Richard II.,* ii. 2.

[5] *Hang the bell about the cat's necke.*

In SKELTON'S *Colyn Clout,* circa 1518.

>   But, quoth one Mouse unto the rest,
>   Which of us all dare be so stout
>   To hang the bell cats neck about ?
>   If here be any, let him speake.
>   Then all replide, We are too weake :
>   The stoutest Mouse and tallest Rat
>   Doe tremble at a grim-fac'd Cat.
>   *Diogines Lanthorne,* 1607.

And for to win this pray, though the cost be mine,

Let us present him with a bottle of wine.

It is to give him, (quoth I), as much almes or neede,

As *cast water in Tems,* or as good a deede

As it is *to helpe a dogge over a stile.*

Then goe we, (quoth he), we leese time all this while.

To follow his fancie we went togither,

And toward night yester night when we came thither,

She was within, but he was yet abrode.

And streight as she saw me *she sweld like a tode,*

Pattring the divels Pater noster to her selfe.

God never made a more crabbed elfe !

She bad him welcome, but the worse for me ;

This knave comth a begging by me, thought she.

I smeld her out, and *had her streight in the winde.*

She may abide no beggers of any kinde.

They be both greedy guts all given to get,

They care not how : *all is fish that comth to net.*[6]

They know no end of their good : nor beginning

Of any goodnes, such is wretched winning.

Hunger droppeth even out of both their noses.

---

[6] *All is fish that comth to net.*
   But now (aye me) the glasing christal glasse
   Doth make us thinke that realmes and townes are rych,
   Where favor sways the sentence of the law,
   Where al is fishe that cometh to net.
                    GASCOIGNE'S *Steele Glas,* 1575.

She goeth broken shoone and torne hoses.

But *who is worse shod than the shoomakers wife,*[7]

With shops full of new shooes all her life ?

Or *who will doe lesse, than they that may doe most ?*

And namely of her I can no way make boste.

She is *one of them to who God bad hoe.*[8]

She will all have, and will right nought forgoe.

She will not *part with the paring of her nayles.*

She toyleth continually for avayles.

Which life she hath so long kept in ure,

That for no life she would make change, be sure.

But this lesson learnd I ere I was yeares seaven,

They that be in hell weene there is none other heaven.

She is nothing fayre, but she is ill favourd ;

And no more unclenely than unsweet savourd.

---

[7] *Who is worse shod than the shoomakers wife ?*

This may be compared with another proverb touching the cobbler's craft, now probably obsolete :—

Heere are the tenne precepts to be observed in the art of scolding : therefore let not the cobler wade above his slipper. The cobler above his slipper, said Chubb, hee is a knave that made that proverb.—*Fearefull and lamentable Effects of two dangerous Comets,* by SIMON SNEL-KNAVE, 1591.

[8] *Hoe* or *whoe* means a stop or limit, from the well-known exclamation used in arresting the attention of a person. Out of this sprang the phrase *out of all hoe*, meaning out of all bounds, beyond restraint.

For he once loved the fair maid of Fresingfield out of all hoe. —GREENE'S *Fryer Bacon.*

But hackney men[9] say at mangie hacknies hyre,

A scald horse is good enough for a scabd squyre.

He is a knuckilbonyard very meete

To match a minion neither fayre nor sweete.

He winkth with the tone eye and looketh with the tother.

I will not trust him though he were my brother.

He hath a poyson wit and all his delite

Is to give taunts and checks of most spitefull spite.

In that house commonly, such is the cast,

A man shall as soone breake his necke as his fast;

And yet now such a gid did her head take,

That more for my mates then for manners sake,

We had bread and drinke, and a cheese very great;

But *the greatest crabs be not all the best meate.*

For her crabbed cheese, with all the greatnes,

Might well abide the fineness or sweetnes.

Anon he came in.   And when he us saw,

---

[9] *Hackney men* at this date are understood to mean proprietors of horses lent for hire ; " a hackney " being the name for a saddle-horse. It was not until the reign of Charles I. that the title was transferred to the drivers of vehicles, the year 1625 being the date of the first appearance of hackney coaches in the streets of London. They were then only twenty in number, but the innovation occasioned an outcry which we find reflected in the pages of a then popular author :—

The world runs on wheeles. The hackney-men, who were wont to have furnished travellers in all places with fitting and service-able horses for any journey, (by the multitude of coaches) are un-

To my companion kindly he did draw,

And a well favour'd welcome to him he yeelds,

Bidding me welcome strangely over the fields,

With these words ; Ah yong man, I know your matter,

By my faith you come to looke in my watter :

And for my comfort to your consolation,

Ye would, by my purse, give me a purgation ;

But I am laxative enough there otherwise.

This, (quoth this yong man), contrary doth rise ;

For he is purse sick, and lackth a Phisition,

And hopeth upon you in some condition,

Not by purgation, but by restorative,

To strength his weaknes, to keepe him alive.

I cannot, (quoth he), for though it be my lot

To have speculation, yet I practise not.

I *see much, but I say little, and doe lesse,*

In this kind of Phisicke.   And what would ye gesse,

Shall I consume my selfe to restore him now ?

Nay, *backare, (quoth Mortimer to his Sow)* ;[10]

---

done by the dozens, and the whole commonwealth most abomin-
ably jaded, that in many places a man had as good to ride on a
wooden post, as to poast it upon one of those hunger-starv'd
hirelings.—TAYLOR'S *Works*, 1630.

[10] *Backare, (quoth Mortimer to his Sow)*.

The allusion is lost, but the phrase would seem to have the
meaning of " to recede," " to go back."

> *Gremio.* Saving your tale, Petruchio, I pray,
> Let us, that are poor petitioners, speak too :
> Baccare ! you are marvellous forward.

He can, before this time, no time assine,

In which he hath laid downe one peny by mine,

That ever might either make me bite or sup ;

And bir Lady, free[nd]! *nought lay downe, nought take up.*

Ka mee, ka thee ;[11] *one good turne asketh another.*

Nought woon by the tone, nought woon by the tother.

To put me to cost thou camst halfe a score miles,

Out of thine owne nest to seeke me in these out yles ;

Where thou wilt not step over a straw, I thinke,

To win me the worth of one draught of drinke,

No more than I have wonne of all thy whole stocke.

I have been common Jacke [12] to all that whole flocke ;

When ought was to doe I was common hackney.

Folke call on the horse that will carry alwey ;

But evermore *the common horse is worse shod.*

Desert and reward be oft times things far od.

At end *I might put my winning in mine eye,*

And see never the worse,[13] for ought I wan them by.

---

[11] *Ka mee, ka thee.*

Skelton sayde then : Why, fellowe, haste thou hurt my mare ?
Yea, sayde the hostler, ka me, ka thee : yf she dose hurte me,
I wyll displease her.—*Merie Tales of* SKELTON, 1567.

[12] *Common Jacke.*

Jack is a familiar appellation for anything rather disparag-
ingly spoken of. In the *Taming of the Shrew,* Katharine calls
her music-master "a twangling jacke," and in *Richard III.* we
have "silken, sly insinuating jacks."

[13] *I might put my winning in mine eye, &c.*

This expression is found Latinized in a letter of Erasmus,

And now without them, I live here at staves end,

Where I need not borow, nor will I lend.

It is good to beware by other mens harmes ;

But thy taking of thine aulter in thine armes

Teacheth other to beware of their harmes by thine.

Thou hast stricken the ball under the line.

I pray you, (quoth I), pitie me a poore man,

With somewhat till I may worke as I can.

Toward your working, (quoth he), ye make such
        tastings,

As approve you to be none of the hastings.

Ye *run to worke in haste as nine men held yee ;*

But whensoever ye to worke must yelde yee,

If your meet-mate and you meete together,

Then shall we see two men beare a fether ;

Recompensing former loytring life loose,

As did *the pure penitent who stole a goose*

And stack downe a fether.   And where old folke tell,

---

circa 1500.   He is speaking of want of generosity in a certain
Cardinal, of whom he says :—

Episcopo Leodiensi nunc Cardinali, cui inscripsimus Epistolas
ad Corinthios, cui libellum inauratum misimus, cui donavimus
duo volumina Novi Testamenti in membranis non ineleganter
adornata neque pretii mediocris ut libenter debemus pro splen-
didis promissis, quæ non semel obtutit : ita non est, quod illi pro
donato teruncio gratias agamus.   Tantum donavit, quantum si
incidat in oculum quamvis tenerum nihil tormenti sit allaturum :
id ipse non inficiabitur.

That *evill gotten goods never proveth well;*

Ye will truly get, and true gettings well keepe,

Till time ye be *as rich as a new shorne sheepe.*[14]

How be it *when thrift and you fell first at a fray,*

You played the man, for ye made thrift run away.

So helpe me God, in my poore opinion,

A man might make a play of this minion,

And faine no ground, but take tales of his owne frends.[15]

I sucke not this out of my owne fingers ends.

And sinse ye were wed, although I nought gave you,

Yet pray I for you, God and saint Luke save you.

---

[14] *As rich as a new shorne sheepe.*

> The nexte that came was a coryar
> And a cobelar, his brother,
> As ryche as a new shorne shepe.
>> *Cocke Lorelles Bote*, circa 1510.

[15] *A man might make a play, &c.*

The meaning of this passage is that a dramatist who represented such a character on the stage, would fill the house without a free list, making even his own friends pay.

The "ground" was that part of a theatre corresponding to the "pit" of the present day, and the pitites were consequently called "groundlings."

The stage curtains be artificially drawn, and so covertly shrouded that the squint-eyed groundling may not peep in.— *Lady Alimony*, i. 1.

The price of admission was one penny.

> Tut, give me the penny, give me the penny—
> Let me have a good ground.
>> BEN JONSON, *Case is Alter'd.*

And here is all. For what should I further wade?
I was neither of Court nor of Counsaile made.
And it is, as I have learned in listening,
A poore dog, that is not worth the whistling.
A day ere I was wed, I bad you, (quoth I).
Scarborough warning I had (quoth he), whereby
I kept me thence, to serve thee according;
And now if this nights lodging and bording
May ease thee, and rid me from any more charge;
Then welcome, or els get thee streight at large.
For of further reward, marke how I bost me,
In case as ye shall yeeld me as ye cost me,
So shall ye cost me as ye yeeld me likewise;
Which is, a thing of nought rightly to surmise.
Herewithall his wife to make up my mouth,
Not onely her husbands taunting tale avouth,
But thereto deviseth to cast in my teeth
Checks and choking oysters. And when she seeth
Her time to take up, to shew my fare at best;
Ye see your fare, (sayd she), set your hart at rest.
Fare ye well, (quoth I), how ever I fare now,
And well mote ye fare both, when I dine with you.
Come, goe we hence friend, (quoth I to my mate),
And now will I make a crosse on this gate.
And I, (quoth he), crosse thee quite out of my booke,
Since thou art crosse sailde, avale unhappie hooke.

By hooke or crooke[16] nought could I win there : men say,

He that comth every day shall have a cocknay ;

He that cometh now and then, shall have a fat hen.

But I gat not so much in comming seeld when,

As a good hens fether, or a poore egshell.

As good play for nought as worke for nought, folke tell.

Well well, (quoth he), we be but where we were,

Come what come would, I thought ere we came there,

That *if the worst fell, we could have but a nay.*

There is no harme done, man, in all this fray ;

Neither pot broken, nor water spilt.

Farewell he, (quoth I), I will as soone be hilt,

As *waite againe, for the moonshine in the watter.*

---

[16] *By hooke or crooke.*

The phrase derives its origin from the custom of certain manors where tenants are authorized to take fire-bote *by hook or by crook;* that is, so much of the underwood as may be cut with a crook, and so much of the loose timber as may be collected from the boughs by means of a hook.

The story of the two arbitrators Judge Hook and Judge Crook, who sat to decide rival claims to property after the Great Fire of London, is of course entirely fallacious.

One of the earliest instances that can be cited is from one of JOHN WYCLIFFE'S *Controversial Tracts,* written circa 1370 :—

þei sillen sacramentis, as ordris, and oþere spiritualte, as halwyng of auteris, of churchis, and churche ȝerdis ; and compellen men to bie alle þis wiþ hok or crok.

Again, in SKELTON'S *Colin Clout,* 1520 :—

> Nor will suffer this boke,
> By hooke or by crooke,
> Prynted for to be.

But is not this a pretie piked matter ?

To disdaine me, who much of the world hoordeth not,

As he doth, *it may rime but it accordeth not.*[17]

She *fometh like a bore*, the beast should seeme bolde ;

For she is *as fierce as a Lion of Cotsolde.*[18]

She frieth in her owne grease,[19] but as for my part,

If she be angrie, beshrew her angrie hart !

Friend, (quoth he), he may shew wisedome at will,

That with angrie hart can hold his tongue still.

Let patience grow in your garden alway.

Some loose or od end will come, man, some one day,

From some friend, either in life or at death.

Death, (quoth I), take we that time to take a breath,

Then graffe we a greene graffe on a rotten roote ;

---

[17] *It may rime, but it accordeth not.*

  It may wele ryme but it accordith nought.
    MS. poem by LYDGATE, " *On Inconstancy.*"

[18] *As fierce as a Lion of Cotsolde.*

DAVIES, in one of his *Epigrams*, has :—

  Carlus is as furious as a lyon of *Cotsold.*

Again, in the play of *Sir John Oldcastle :*—

  You stale old ruffian, you lion of Cotsolde.

The Cotswold hills in Gloucestershire were famous on account of the number of sheep fed there ; hence a Cotswold lion meant a Cotswold sheep.

[19] *She frieth in her owne grease.*

  But certeynly I made folk such chere .
  That in his owne grees I made him frie.
    CHAUCER, *Prologue of Wyf of Bathe.*

Prince Bismarck's recent application of the saying is well known.

Who waite for dead men shoen shall goe long barefoote.[20]

Let passe, (quoth he), and let us be trudging,

Where some nappie ale is and soft sweet lodging.

Be it, (quoth I), but I would very faine eate,

At breakfast and dinner I eate little meate,

And *two' hungrie meales make the third a glutton.*

We went where we had boyld beefe and bakte mutton,

Whereof I fed me *as full as a tunne ;*

And a bed were we ere the clock had nine runne.

Earely we rose, in haste to get away,

And to the hostler this morning by day,

This fellow calde. What how fellow, thou knave,

I pray thee let me and my fellow have

A haire of the dog that bit us[1] last night.

And bitten were we both to the braine aright.

---

[20] *Who waite for dead men shoen shall goe long barefoote.*

Nicholas. You may speake when ye are spoken to, and keepe your winde to coole your pottage. Well, well, you are my maister's sonne, and you looke for his lande ; but they that hope for dead mens shoes may hap go barefoote.—*Two angry Women of Abington,* 1599.

[1] *A haire of the dog that bit us.*

In old receipt books we find it invariably advised that an inebriate should drink sparingly in the morning some of the same liquor which he had drunk to excess over-night.

Pepys records, under April 3, 1661 :—

Up among my workmen, my head akeing all day from last night's debauch. At noon dined with Sir W. Batten and Pen, who would have me drink two good draughts of sack to-day, to cure me of my last night's disease, which I thought strange, but I think find it true.

We saw each other drunke in the good ale glas,
And so did each one each other that there was,
Save one, but old men say that are skild
A hard foughten field where no man scapeth unkild.
The reckning reckned, he needes would *pay the shot*,[2]
And needes he must for me, for I had it not.'
This done we shooke hands, and parted in fine ;
He into his way, and I into mine.
But this journey was quite out of my way,
Many kinsfolke and few friends, some folke say ;
But I finde many kinsfolke, and friend not one.
Folke say, it hath been sayd many yeares since gone ;
Prove thy friend ere thou have need ; but in deede,
A friend is never knowne till a man have neede.
Before I had neede, my most present foes
Seemed my most friends, but thus the world goes.
Every man basteth the fat hog, we see ;
But the leane shall burne ere he basted bee.
As saith this sentence, oft and long sayd before,
He that hath plentie of goods shall have more ;
He that hath but a little he shall have lesse.
He that hath right nought, right nought shall possesse.
Thus having right nought and would somewhat obtaine,
With right nought, (quoth he), I am returned againe.

---

[2] *Pay the shot.*
Well at your will ye shall be furnisht. But now a jugling
tricke to pay the shot.—*Kind Harts Dreame*, 1592.

CHAPTER XII.

SURELY, (quoth I), ye have in this time thus
　　worne,
　　Made a long harvest for a little corne.
Howbeit, comfort your selfe with this old text,
That telth us; *when bale is hekst, boote is next.*[3]
Though every man may not sit in the chaire,
Yet alway the grace of *God is worth a faire.*
Take no thought in case, God is where he was,
And put case[4] in povertie all your life pas.

---

[3] *When bale is hekst, boote is next.*

Equivalent to saying that when things are at worst they begin
to mend.

> When bale is greatest, then is bote a nie bore.
> > CHAUCER, *Testament of Love.*

> "When the bale is hest,
> 　Thenne is the bote nest,"
> 　Quoth Hendyng.
> > *Proverbs of Hendyng,* MS. circa 1320.

[4] *Put case.*

An idiomatic expression used frequently in an argument, as,—

Put case there be three brethren, John-a-Nokes, John-a-Nash
and John-a-Stile.—*Returne from Parnassus,* 1606.

G

Yet povertie and poore degree, taken well,

Feedth on this ; *he that never climbde never fell.*

And some case at some time shewth preefe somewhere,

That *riches bring oft harme and ever feare,*

Where povertie passeth without grudge of greefe.

What man ! *the begger may sing before the theefe.*

And *who can sing so merrie a note,*

As may he that cannot change a grote ?

Ye, (quoth he), *beggers may sing before theeves,*

And weepe before true men, lamenting their greeves.

Some say, and I feele, *hunger pearceth stone wall.*[5]

Meate, nor yet money to buy meate withall,

Have I not so much as may hunger defend

Fro my wife and me.   Well, (quoth I), God will send

Time to provide for time, right well ye shall see.

God send that provision in time, (sayd hee).

And thus seeming welnie wearie of his life,

The poore wretch went to his like poore wretched wife.

---

[5] *Hunger pearceth stone wall.*

Menenius. But, I beseech you,
What says the other troop ?
   Marcius. They are dissolved : Hang 'em !
They said, they were an-hungry ; sigh'd forth proverbs ;—
That, hunger broke stone walls ; that, dogs must eat ;
That, meat was made for mouths, that, the Gods sent not
Corn for the rich man only :—With these shreds
They vented their complainings.   *Coriolanus,* i. 1.

From wantonnes to wretchednes, brought on their knees ;
Their hearts full heavie, *their heads full of bees.*[6]
And after this a month, or somewhat lesse,
Their Landlord came to their house to make a stresse
For rent, *to have kept Bayard in the stable.*
But that to win, any power was unable.
For though *it be ill playing with short daggers,*
Which meaneth, that every wise man staggers,
In earnest or boord to be busie or bold
With his biggers or betters, yet this is tolde ;
Where as *nothing is, the King must lose his right.*
And thus, King or Keyser must have set them quight.
But warning to depart thence they needed none ;
For ere the next day the birds were flowne each one,
To seeke service ; of which where the man was sped,
The wife could not speede, but maugre her hed,
She must seeke elsewhere. For either there or nie,
Service for any suite she none could espie.
All folke thought them not onely too lither,
To linger both in one house togither.

---

[6] *Their heads full of bees.*

Means to project schemes ; thus differing from the phrase
"to have a bee in one's bonnet," which is generally intended to
denote a mild form of craziness.

> But, Wyll, my maister hath bees in his head.
> *Damon and Pithias,* 1571.

But also dwelling nie under their wings,
Under their noses they might convey things,
Such as were neither too heavie nor too hot,
More in a month then they their master got
In a whole yeare.   Whereto folke further weying,
Receive each of other in their conveying,
Might be worst of all.   For this proverb preeves;
Where there be no receivers, there be no theeves.[7]
Such hap here hapt, that common dread of such guiles
Drove them and keepth them asunder many miles.
Thus though love decree departure death to bee,
Yet *povertie parteth fellowship*, we see;
And doth those two true lovers so dissever,
That meete shall they seeld, when, or haply never.
And thus by love without regard of living,
These twaine have wrought each others ill chiving.
And love hath so lost them the love of their friends,
That I thinke them lost; and thus this tale ends.

---

[7] *Where there be no receivers, there be no theeves.*

And it is a comon sayinge, ware there no ryceyver there shoulde be no thefe.   So ware there no stewes, there shulde not so many honeste mennes doughters rune awaye from there fathers and playe the whores as dothe. — *A Christen exhortation unto customable swearers*, 1575.

CHAPTER XIII.

A H sir, (sayd my friend), when men must needes
marry,
I see now how wisedome and haste may varry;
Namely where they wed for love altogither.
I would for no good, but I had come hither.
Sweet beautie with soure beggerie? nay, I am gon
To the wealthie withered widow, by Saint John.
What yet in all haste, (quoth I). Yea, (quoth he),
For she hath substance enough. And ye see,
That lacke is the losse of these two yong fooles.
Know ye not, (quoth I), that after wise mens schooles
A man should heare all parts ere he judge any?
Why are ye that, (quoth he)? For this, (quoth I);
I tolde you, when I this began that I would
Tell you of two couples. And I having told
But of the tone, ye be streight starting away,
As I of the tother had right nought to say,
Or as your selfe of them right nought would heare.
Nay not allso, (quoth he), but since I thinke cleare,
There can no way appeare so painfull a life,
Betweene your yong neighbour and his old rich wife,
As this tale in this yong poore couple doth show,
And that the most good or least ill ye know.

To take at end, I was at beginning bent,

With thankes for this and your more paine to prevent,

Without any more matter now revolved,

I take this matter here cleerely resolved.

And that ye herein award me to forsake,

Beggerly beautie, and riveld riches take.

That's just, if the *halfe shall judge the whole,* (quoth I);

But yet heare the whole, the whole wholly to try.

To it, (quoth he), then I pray you by and by.

We will dine first, (quoth he), it is noone by.

We may as well, (quoth he), dine when this is done ;

The longer forenoone, the shorter afternoone.

All comth to one, and thereby men have gest ;

Alway the longer east, the shorter west.

We have had, (quoth I), before ye came, and sin,

Weather, meete to sette paddocks abroode in,

Raine more then enough ; and *when all shrews have
        dinde,*

Change from foule weather to faire is oft enclinde.

And all the shrews in this part, saving one wife

That must dine with us, have dinde, paine of my life.

Now if good change of ill weather be depending

Upon her diet, what were mine offending,

To keepe the woman any longer fasting ?

If ye, (quoth he), set all this far casting

For common wealth, as it appeareth a cleere case,

Reason would your will should and shall take place.

PART II.

CHAPTER I.

*D INNER cannot be long where dainties
    want,
    Where coyne is not cōmon, cōmons must
    be scant,*

In poste pase we past from potage to cheese,
And yet this man cride, alas what time we leese.
He would not let us pause after our repaste,
But apart he pluckt me streight, and in all haste,
As I of this poore yong man and poore yong maide,
Or more poore yong wife, the foresaid words had saide,
So praieth he me now the processe may be told,
Betweene th'other yong man, and the rich widowe old.
If yee lacke that, (quoth I), away ye must winde,
With your whole errand, and halfe th' answer behinde.
Which thing to doe, sens hast thereto shewth you loth

And to hast your going, the day away goth,
And that time lost, againe we cannot win,
Without more losse of time, this tale I begin.

In this late olde widowe, and then olde new wife,
Age and appetite fell at a strong strife.
Her lust was as yong as her lims were olde.
The day of her wedding, liken one to be solde,
She set out her selfe in fine apparell.
She was made like a beere pot, or a barrell.
A crooked hookde nose, beetle browde, blere eyed.
Many men wisht, for beautifyng that bryde,
Her waste to be gyrde in, and for a boone grace,
Some well favourd visor, on her ill favourd face.
But with visorlike visage, such as it was,
Shee smirkt, and she smilde ; but so lisped this las,
That folke might have thought it done onely alone
Of wantonnesse, had not her teeth been gone.
Upright as a candell standth in a socket,
Stoode she that day, *so simper decocket.*[8]
Of auncient fathers she tooke no cure nor care,

---

[8] *So simper decocket.*
             And gray russet rocket
             With simper the cocket.
                      SKELTON, *The Tunnyng of Elynoure*
                                Rummyng, 1520.
The word means a coquettish girl.

She was to them, *as koy as Croker's mare.*

She tooke th' entertainment of the yong men

All in daliaunce, *as nice as a nunnes hen.*[9]

I suppose that day her eares might well glow,

For all the towne talkt of her hie and low.

One sayd ; a well favourd olde woman she is ;

The divell she is, saide another ; and to this,

In came the third, with his five egges, and sayde ;

Fiftie yere a goe I knew her a trym mayde.

What ever she were then, (said one), she is now

To become a bryde, *as meete as a sow*

---

[9] *As nice as a nunnes hen.*

This proverb appears to have been in use a century previous
to Heywood.

> Women, women, love of women,
> Make bare purs with some men.
> Some be nyse as a nonne hene,
>   Yet al thei be not soo ;
> Some be lewde, some all be schrewde,
>   Go schrewes wher thei goo.
>   *Satirical Verses on Women,* 1462.

I knewe a priest that was as nice as a Nonnes Henne.—
WILSON'S *Arte of Rhetorique,* 1562.

Another virtue is ascribed to this kind of poultry by the old
writers,—

> I have the taught dyvysyon between
> Frende of effect, and frende of countenaunce ;
> The nedeth not the gall of none hen
> That cureth eyen.
>   *Proverbes of Lydgate,* circa 1520.

To beare a saddle.   She is in this mariage
As comely as is a cowe in a cage.
Gup, with a galde backe, gill, come up to supper.
What, mine olde mare would have a new crupper!
And now mine olde hat must have a new band!
Well (quoth one) glad is he that hath her in hand;
A goodly mariage she is, I heare say.
She is so, (quoth one), were the woman away.
Well, (quoth another), fortune this moveth;
And in this case, *every man as he loveth*
Quoth the good man, when that he kist his cowe.
That kisse, (quoth one), doth well here, by God a vowe;
But how can she give a kisse sowre or sweete?
Her chin and her nose within halfe an inche meete.
God is no botcher, sir, sayd another;
He shapeth all parts, as eche part may fit other.
Well, (quoth one), wisely; let us leave this scanning.
God speede, *be as be may is no banning.*
That shalbe, shalbe ; and with god's grace they shall
Doe well, and that they so may, wish wee all.

This wonder, (as wonders last), *lasted nine daies.*[10]
Which done, and all gests of this feast gone their waies,

---

[10] *This wonder . . . lasted nine daies.*
The reason for assigning nine days as the period of duration is

Ordinary houshold this man streight began
Very sumptuously, which he might well doe than.
What he would have, he might have; his wife was set
In such dotage of him, that faire words did fet
Gromel-seede plenty; and pleasure to prefer,
Shee made much of him, and he mockt much of her.
I was, (as I said), much there, and most of all,
The first month, in which time such kindnesse did fall
Betweene these two counterfaite turtle burds.
To see his sweete looke, and heare her sweete wurds,
And to thinke wherefore they both put both in ure,
It would have made a horse breake his halter sure.
All the first fortnight their tickyng might have tought
Any yong couple their love trickes to have wrought.
Some laught, and sayd; *all thing is gay that is greene.*
Some thereto said; *new brome swepth cleene.*
But since *all thing is the woorse for the wearing,*
Decay of cleane sweeping folke had in fearing.
And in deede, ere two monthes away were crept,
And her biggest bagges into his bosome swept:

---

not ascertained, but the proverb is traced to the works of
Chaucer.

> Eke wonder last but nine deies never in town.
>> CHAUCER, *Troilus and Creseide.*

A book on any subject by a peasant, or a peer, is no longer so
much as a nine-days wonder.—ASCHAM'S *Schoole-master.*

Where love had appeared in him to her away
Hot as a toste, it grewe *cold as kay*.[11]
Hee at meate carving her, and none els before,
Now carved he to all but her, and to her no more.
Where her words seemde hony, by his smiling cheare,
Now are they mustard, he frowneth them to heare.
And when shee sawe sweete sauce began to ware sowre,
She waxt as sowre as he, and as well could lowre.
So turned they their tippets[12] by way of exchaunge,
From laughing to lowring, and taunts did so raunge ;
That in plaine termes, plaine truth to you to utter,
They two *agreed like two cats in a gutter.*
Mary sir, (quoth he), *by scratching and biting,*
Cats and dogs come together, by folks reciting.
Together by the eares they come, (quoth I), cheerely.
How be it those wordes are not voide here cleerely ;
For in one state they twaine could not yet settle,

---

[11] *Cold as kay.*

> Poor key-cold figure of a holy king.
>
> > *Richard III*. i. 2.

[12] *So turned they their tippets.*

"To turn tippet" meant, and means, to make a complete change. Now it is applied to one going over to an adversary ; formerly it was usually said of a maid becoming a wife.

> Another Bridget ; one that for a face
> Would put down Vesta ;
> You to turn tippet !
>
> > BEN JONSON, *Case is Altered.*

But wavering as the winde ; *in docke, out nettle.*[13]

Now in, now out ; now here, now there ; now sad,

Now mery ; now hie, now lowe ; now good, now bad.

In which unstedy sturdy stormes streinable,

To know how they both were irrefreynable,

Marke how they fell out, and how they fell in,

At end of a supper shee did thus begin.

---

[13] *In docke, out nettle.*

A charm for a nettle sting which had early passed into a proverb expressive of inconstancy.

Ye wete well Ladie eke (quoth I) that I have not plaid racket, Nettle in, Docke out, and with this the weathercocke waved.— CHAUCER, *Testament of Love.*

> Is this my in dock, out nettle ?
> MIDDLETON, *More Dissemblers besides Women.*

CHAPTER II.

USBAND, (quoth shee), I would we were in
our nest;
When the belly is full, the bones would be
at rest.
So soone uppon supper, (sayd he), no question,
Sleepe maketh ill and unholsome digestion.
By that diet a great disease once I gat ;
And *burnt child fire dredth ;* [14] I will beware of that.
What a post of phisicke, (sayd shee), yee a post.
And *from post to piller,*[15] wife, I have been tost

---

[14] *Burnt child fire dredth.*

Timon. Why urge yee me ? my hart doth boyle with heate,
And will not stoope to any of your lures :
A burnt childe dreads the ffyre.—*Timon,* circa 1590.

> So that child withdraweth is hond,
> From the fur ant the brond,
>   That hath byfore bue brend.
> " Brend child fur dredth,"
>   Quoth Hendyng.
> *Proverbs of Hendyng,* MS. circa 1320.

[15] *From post to piller.*

Meletya. Sister, is not your waighting-wench rich ?
Celia. Why, sister, why ?
Meletya. Because she can flatter, Pree-thee call her not.   She

By that surfet.   And I feele a little fyt
Even now, by former attempting of it.
Whereby, except I shall seeme to leave my wit
Before it leave me, I must now leave it.
I thanke God, (quoth shee), I never yet felt paine
To goe to bed timely, but rising againe,
Too soone in the morning, hath mee displeased.
And I, (quoth he), have been more diseased
By earely liyng downe, then by early rising.
But thus differ folke lo, in exercysing ;
That one may not, an other may.
Use maketh maistry ; and men many times say,
That one loveth not, an other doth ; which hath sped,
All meates to be eaten and all maides to be wed.
Haste ye to bed now, and rise ye as readie,
While I rise earely and come to bed late.
Long lying warme in bed is holesome, (quoth shee).
While the leg warmeth, the boote harmeth,[16] (quoth he).
Well, (quoth shee), *he that doth as most men do,*
Shalbe least wondred on, and take any two,

---

has twenty-four houres to maddam yet, Come you, you prate,
yfaith, Ile tosse you from post to piller !—MARSTON'S *What you
Will,* 1607.

[16] *While the leg warmeth, the boote harmeth.*
        Whan the scho harmt the fot war . . .
                        MS. Harleian, circa 1490.

That be man and wife in all this whole towne,

And most part together they rise and lie downe.

When birds shall roost, (quoth he), at viii, ix, or ten,

Who shall appoynt their houre, the cock or the hen ?

The hen, (quoth shee) ; the cocke, (quoth he) ; *just,*
       (quoth she),

As Jermans lips.[17]   It shall prove more just (quoth he).

Then prove I, (quoth shee), the more foole far away ;

But *there is no foole to the old foole,*[18] folke say.

Ye are wise inough, (quoth he), if ye keepe ye warme.

To be kept warme, and for none other harme,

Nor for much more good, I tooke you to wed.

I tooke not you, (quoth he), night and day to bed.

Her carraine carkas, (sayd hee), is so cold,

Because shee is aged, and somewhat too old,

---

[17] *Just . . . as Jermans lips.*

As just as German's lips, which came not together by nine mile.—LATIMER'S *Remaines.*

Agree like Dogge and Catte, and meete as just as Germans lippes.—GOSSON'S *Schole of Abuse.*

[18] *No foole to the old foole.*

Comedie upon comedie he shall have ; a morall, a historie, a tragedie, or what he will.   One shal be called the *Doctor's dumpe* . . . and last *a pleasant Enterlude of No Foole to the Olde Foole*, with a jigge at the latter end in English hexameters of *O Neighbour Gabriell! ! and his wooing of Kate Cotton.*—NASH'S *Have with you to Saffron Walden*, 1596.

That shee kilth mee. I doe but *roste a stone*,[19]
In warming her. And shall not I save one,
As shee would save an other ? yes by seint Johne.
A syr, (quoth shee), mary this geare is alone.
Who that worst may shall holde the candell ; I see ;
I must warme bed for him should warme it for mee.
This medicine thus ministred is sharpe and cold ;
But *all things that is sharpe is short*, folke have told.
This trade is now b[e]gun, but if it holde on,
Then farewell my good dayes, they will be soone gon.
Gospell in thy mouth, (quoth hee), this strife to breake !
How be it, *all is not Gospell that thou doest speake.*
But what neede we lumpe out love at ones lashing,
As wee should now shake handes ? what ! soft for
     dashing.
The fayre lasteth all the yeare. We be new knit,
And so late met, that I feare *wee part not yit;*
Quoth the baker to the pilory. Which thing,
From distemperate fonding, temperance may bring.
And this reason to aide and make it more strong,

---

[19] *Roste a stone.*

    They may garlicke pill
    Cary sackes to the mil
    Or pescoddes they may shil
    Or els go roste a stone.
      SKELTON'S *Why come ye not to Court ?* 1520.

H

Old wise folke say ; *love me litle, love me long.*[20]
I say little, (sayd shee), but I thinke more ;
Thought is free.[21] *Ye leane,* (quoth he), *to the wrong shore.*
Brauling booted not, he was not that night bent
To play the bridegroome. Alone to bed shee went,
This was their beginning of jar. Hòw be it,
For a beginning, this was a feate fit,
And but a fleabiting to thàt did ensew.
The worst is behinde. We come not where it grewe.
How say you, (sayd he to me), by my wife ?
The divell hath cast a bone, (sayd I), to set strife
Betweene you, but it were a folly for me,
To put my hand betweene the barke and the tree,
Or to put my finger too far in the fire,
Betweene you, and lay my credite in the mire.

---

[20] *Love me litle, love me long.*

Bellamira. Come, gentle Ithamore, lie in my lap.
Ithamore. Love me little, love me long ; let music rumble,
Whilst I in thy incony lap do tumble.
MARLOWE'S *Jew of Malta,* iv.

[21] *Thought is free.*

Since thought is free, thinke what thou will,
O troubled hart to ease thy paine !
Thought unrevealed can do no evill,
Bot wordes past out, cummes not againe.
Be cairefull aye for to invent
The waye to gett thy owen intent.
Poem by James I.—MS. Add. 24,195.

To meddle litle for mee it is best ;

For *of litle medling commeth great rest.*[22]

Yes, yee may meddle, (quoth hee), to make hir wise,

Without taking harme, in giving your advice.

She knoweth mee not yet, but if shee ware to wilde,

I shall make hir know, *an old knave is no childe.*

Slugging in bed with her is worse than watching.

I promise you, *an olde sacke asketh much patching.*

Well, (quoth I), to morowe I will to my beades,

To pray, that as ye both will so ake your heades,

And in meane time my aking head to cease,

I will couch a hogs head.   Quoth he, when yee
    please.

Wee parted, and this, within a day or twayne,

Was rakte up in th' ashes and covered agayne.

---

[22] *Of litle medling commeth great rest.*

> Payne the not eche croked to redresse
> In truste of her that turneth as a ball :
> Grete reste stande in lytell besynesse,
> Beware also to sporne against a wall.
> > *Proverbes of Lydgate.*

CHAPTER III.

HESE two dayes past, hee sayd to mee, when
          ye will,
    Come chat at home, all is well ; *Jacke shall
          have Gill.*
Who had the worse end of the staffe, (quoth I), now ?
Shall the mayster weare a breeche,[1] or none, say you ?
I trust the sowe will no more so deepe wroote ;
But if shee doe, (quoth he), you must set in foote :
And whom yee see out of the way, or shoote wide,
Over shoote not your selfe any side to hide.
But shoote out some wordes, if she be too hot.
Shee may say, (quoth I), *a fooles bolt is soone shot.*[2]

---

[1] *Weare a breeche.*
> All women be suche,
> Thoughe the man bere the breeche,
> They wyll be ever checkemate.
>> *The Boke of Mayd Emlyn,* 1515.

[2] *A fooles bolt is soone shot.*
> Sot is sot, and that is sene ;
> For he wel speke wordes grene,
>   Er ther hue buen rype.
> " Sottes bolt is sone shote,"
>   Quoth Hendyng.
>> *Proverbs of Hendyng,* MS. circa 1320.

Yee will mee to a thankelesse office heere,

And a busy officer I may appeere ;

And Jacke out of office[3] she may bid me walke,

And thinke me *as wise as Waltams calfe*,[4] to talke,

Or chat of her charge, having therein nought to do.

How be it, if I see neede, as my part comth too,

Gladly betweene you I will doe my best.

I bid you to dinner, (quoth hee), as no guest,

And bring your poore neighbors on your other side.

I did so.   And streight as th' old Wife us espide,

---

[3] *Jacke out of office.*

For liberalitie is tourned Jacke out of office, and others appointed to have [the custodie.—RICH'S *Farewell to Militarie
Profession*, 1581.

[4] *As wise as Waltams calfe.*

> For Waltham's calves to Tiburne needes must go
> To sucke a bull and meete a butchers axe.
> > *The Braineles blessing of the Bull*, 1571.

In SKELTON'S *Colin Clout*, 1520, an unsanctimonious divine
is thus pourtrayed :

> As wyse as Waltom's calfe,
> Must preche, a Goddes halfe,
> In the pulpyt solempnely ;
> More mete in the pyllory,
> For, by saynt Hyllary,
> He can nothyng smatter
> Of logyke nor scole matter.

Ray gives, "As wise as Walthams calf, that ran nine miles to
suck a bull."

Shee bad us welcome and merrily toward me ;
Greene rushes for this stranger,[5] strew here, (quoth shee),
With this apart she puld me by the sleeve,
Saying in fewe words, my mind to you to meeve ;
So it is, that all our great fray the last night,
Is forgiven and forgotten betweene us quight.
And all fraies by this I trust have taken end ;
For I fully hope my husband will amend.
Well amended, (thought I), when yee both relent,
Not to your owne, but ech to others mendment.
Now if hope faile, (quoth she), and chaunce bring about
Any such breach, whereby wee fall againe out,
I pray you, tel him he is perverse now and than,
And winke on me.   Also hardly, if yee can
Take me in any trip.   Quoth I, I am loth
To meddle commonly.   For as this tale goth ;
Who medleth in all thing, may shoe the gosling.[6]

---

[5] *Greene rushes for this stranger.*

It was usual, before the introduction of carpets, to strew rushes on the floors of dwelling-houses ; and on the entrance of a visitor, hospitality required that they should be renewed.

> Where is this stranger ? Rushes, ladies, rushes :
> Rushes as green as summer for this stranger.
> BEAUMONT AND FLETCHER, *Valentinian,* ii. 4.

[6] *Who medleth in all thing, may shoe the gosling.*

To shoe the goose (gosling here for the sake of rhyme) means simply to perform a work of supererogation.   An inscription on

Well, (quoth shee), your medling herein may be

The winde calme betweene us, when it els might rage.

I will with good will, (quoth I), ill windes to swage,

Spend some winde at need, though I waste wind in
      vaine.

To table we sat, where fine fare did remaine.

Merry we were *as cup and can* could holde,

Each one with each other homely and bolde.

And she for her part, made us cheere heaven hie.

The first part of dinner *merry as a pie.*[7]

But *a scald head is soone broken;* and so they,

As ye shall straight heare, fell at a new frey.

---

one of the stalls of Whalley Church of the date 1434 goes far to
show the antiquity of the proverb :

    Whoso melles of wat men dos,
    Let hym cum hier and shoo the ghos.

And in *Colin Clout*, 1510 :

    What hath lay men to do
    The gray goose for to sho !

In connection with this proverb may be mentioned another
much on the same model, occurring in the *Hundred Mery Talys*,
circa 1525 :

It is as great pyte to se a woman wepe as a gose to go barefote,
and reappearing in a new dress in Sir Walter Scott's novel, "Rob
Roy," where it is thus put into the mouth of Bailie Nicol Jarvie :

It's nae mair ferlie to see a woman greet than to see a goose
gang barefit.

[7] *Merry as a pie.*

Eyre. By the Lord of Ludgate, my Liege, I'll be as merrie as
a Pie.—DECKER'S *Shomakers Holiday*, 1600.

CHAPTER IV

USBAND, (quoth she), ye studie, be merrie
now,
And even as ye thinke now, so come to yow.
Nay not so, (quoth he), for my thought to tell right,
I thinke how you lay groning, wife, all last night. ·
Husband, *a groning horse and a groning wife
Never faile their master*, (quoth she), for my life.
No wife, *a woman hath nine lives like a cat.*
Well, my lambe, (quoth she), ye may pick out of that,
*As soone goth the yong lambe skin to the market
As th' old yewes.*[8] God forbid, wife, ye shall first jet.
I will not jet yet, (quoth she), put no doubting ;
It is a bad sack that will abide no clouting.
And as we oft see, *the looth stake standeth long*,
So *it is an ill stake*, I have heard among,
That cannot stand one yeare in a hedge.
I drinke, (quoth she). Quoth he, I will not pledge.
What neede all this, *a man may love his house well,*

---

[8] *As soone goth the yong lambe skin, &c.*
It is a common saying there do come as many skins of calves
to the market as there do of bulls or kine.—BARCLAY'S *Ship of
Fools.*

Though he ride not on the ridge ; I have heard tell.

What, I weene, (quoth she), *proferd service stinketh.*[9]

But somewhat it is, I see, *when the cat winketh,*

And both her eyen out, but further strife to shunne,

Let the cat winke, and let the mouse runne.

This past, and he cheered us all, but most cheere

On his part, to this fayre yong wife did appeare.

And as he to her cast oft a loving eye,

So cast her husband like eye to his plate by.

Wherewith in a great musing he was brought.

Friend, (quoth the good man), *a peny for your thought ?*[10]

For my thought, (quoth he), that is a goodly dish :

But of troth I thought ; *better to have then wish.*

What, a goodly yong wife, as you have, (quoth he) ?

Nay, (quoth he), gooldly gilt goblets, as here be.

Bir Ladie friends, (quoth I), this maketh a show,

To shew you more unnaturall then the crow ;

---

[9] *Proferd service stinketh.*

In *Vulgaria Slambrigi,* 1510.

[10] *A peny for your thought.*

Me thinke, Euphues, chaunging so your colour upon the so-
deine, you wil soone chaunge your coppie : is your minde on your
meate ? a penny for your thought.

Mistres (quoth he) if you would by al my thoughts at that
price, I should never be wearye of thinking, but seeing it is too
deare, reade it and take it for nothing.—*Euphues. The Anatomy
of Wit,* 1579.

The crow thinkth her owne birds fairest in the wood.[11]
But by your words, (except I wrong understood),
Each others birds or jewels, you doe wey
Above your owne.   True, (quoth the old wife), ye sey.
But my neighbours desire rightly to measure,
Comth of neede, and not of corrupted pleasure ;
And my husbands more of pleasure, than of neede.
Old fish and yong flesh, (quoth he), *doth men best feede.*
And some say ; *change of pasture makth fat calves.*[12]
As for that reason, (quoth she), runneth to halves,
As well for the cow calfe as for the bull.
And though your pasture looke barrenly and dull,
Yet *looke not on the meate, but looke on the man.*
And who so looketh on you, shall shortly skan.

---

[11] *The crow thinkth her owne birds fairest in the wood.*

It must needs be good ground that brings forth such good corne;
When I look on him, methinks him to be evill favoured,
Yet the crowe thinkes her black birds of all other the fairest.

LUPTON'S *All for Money*, 1578.

[12] *Change of pasture makth fat calves.*

Honeysuckle. Now I'm as limber as an ancient that has flourished in the rain, and as active as a Norfolk tumbler.

Boniface. You may see what change of pasture is able to do.

Honeysuckle. It makes fat calves in Romney Marsh, and lean knaves in London, therefore Boniface, keep your ground. God's my pity, my forehead has more crumples than the back part of a counsellor's gown, when another rides upon his necke at the bar.—WEBSTER'S *Westward Hoe.*

Ye may write to your friends that ye are in health ;
But all thing may be suffred saving wealth.
An old said saw ; *itch and ease can no man please.*
Plentie is no daintie ; ye see not your owne ease.
I see, *you cannot see the wood for trees.*[13]
Your lips hang in your light ; but this poore man sees,
Both how blindly *you stand in your owne light,*
And that *you rose on your right side* here right,
And might have *gone further and have fared worse.*
I wot well I might, (quoth he), for the purse ;
But ye be *a babie of Belzabub's bowre.*
Content ye, (quoth she), take the sweet with the sowre ;
Fancy *may boult bran, and make yee take it floure.*
It will not be, (quoth he), should I die this houre,
While this fayre floure flourisheth thus in mine eie.
Yes, it might, (quoth shee), and here this reason whye.

Snow is white, $\Big\}$ And every man lets it lye.
And lieth in the dike.

---

[13] *You cannot see the wood for trees.*

Continued proverbial, being found in an anti-popish tract of the reign of Charles II.

> From him who sees no wood for trees
> And yet is busie as the bees
> From him that's settled on his lees
> And speaketh not without his fees,
> Libera nos.
>
> *A Letany for S. Omers,* 1682.

Pepper is blacke

And hath a good smack. } And every man doth it bie.

Milke, (quoth he), is white, } But all men know it good

And lieth not in the dike. } meate.

Inke is all blacke, } No man will it drinke nor

And hath an ill smacke. } eate.

Thy ryme, (quoth hee), is much elder then mine,

But mine being newer is truer then thine.

Thou likenest now for a vaine advauntage,

White snow to faire youth, blacke pepper to foule age

Which are placed out of place heere by the rood,

Blacke inke is as ill meate, as blacke pepper is good.

And white milke is good meat, as white snow is ill.

But a milke snow white smooth yong skin, who chaunge

 wil

For a pepper inke rough olde withred face?

Though *chaunge bee no robbry* for the chaunged case,

Yet shall that change rob the chaunger of his wit.

For who this case searcheth, shall soone see in it,

That as well agreeth the comparison in these,

As a lyke *to compare* in tast, *chalke and cheese.*[14]

---

[14] *To compare . . . . chalke and cheese.*

 Lo! how they feignen chalk for cheese.

  GOWER'S *Confessio Amantis.*

 Though I have no learning, yet I know chese from chalke.—
John Bon and Mast Person, 1548.

Or a lyke in colour to deeme inke and chalke.

Walke, drab, walke ! Nay, (quoth she), *walke, knave,
      walke;*

Saith that terme.   How be it sir, I say not so.

And lest wee lay a straw here, and even there, ho,

Or else this geare will *breede a pad in the straw.*

If yee hale this way, I will an other way draw.

Here is God in th' ambry, (quoth I).   Quoth hee, nay,

Here is *the devill in th' orologe;*[15] yee may say.

Since this, (quoth I), rather bringeth bale then boote,

Wrap it in the cloth, and tread it under foote.

Ye harpe on the string that geveth no melody.

Your tongs run before your wittes, by saint Antony.

Marke yee, how she *hitteth mee on the thumbes,* (quoth
      hee).

And yee taunt mee tit over thumb, (quoth shee).

Since *tit for tat,*[16] (quoth I), on even hand is set,

Do not these thynges differ as muche as chalcke and chese.—
SHACKLOCK'S *Hatchet of Heresies,* 1565.

> To French and Scots so fayr a taell I tolde,
> That they beleeved whyt chalk and chees was oen.
>   CHURCHYARD'S *Chippes,* 1573.

[15] *The devill in th' orologe.*

In HARMAN'S *Vulgaria,* 1530 :—

> —some for a tryfull pley the devyll in the orloge.

[16] *Tit for tat,* is simply a corruption of *tant pour tant.*

Set the hares head agaynst the goose jeblet.[17]

She is, (quoth he), bent to force you perforce,

To know that *the grey mare is the better horse.*[18]

Shee chopth logyke, to put me to my clargie :

Shee hath *one poynt of a good hauke ; shee is hardy.*

---

[17] *Set the hares head agaynst the goose jeblet.*

    Ide set mine old debts against my new driblets,
    And the hare's foot against the goose giblets.

                  DECKER'S *Shomakers Holiday.*

[18] *The grey mare is the better horse.*

Lord Macaulay observes in his history, (i.—iii.) :—

" Our native horses, though serviceable, were held in small esteem, and fetched low prices. They were valued, one with another, by the ablest of those who computed the national wealth, at fifty shillings each. Foreign breeds were greatly preferred."

And adds in a note :—

" The common proverb, that the grey mare is the better horse, originated, I suspect, in the preference generally given to the grey mares of Flanders over the finest coach horses of England."

Macaulay is writing of the latter half of the seventeenth century. That the proverb had always been associated with the idea of female superiority appears both from Heywood's text, from the Hudibras, and in innumerable later instances.

    What ! shall the graye mayre be the better horse,
    And the wanton styll at home ?

      Pryde and Abuse of Women Now a Dayes, circa 1550.

      When the grey mare's the better horse,
      When o'er the breeches greedy women
      Fight, to extend their vast dominion.

                  Hudibras.

But wife, *the first poynt of hauking is hold fast ;*[1]
And hold ye fast I red you, lest yee bee cast
In your own turne.   Nay shee will *turne the leafe,*[19]
And rather, (quoth I), take as falth in the sheafe
At your handes, and let fall her hold, than be too bolde.
Nay, I will spit in my handes, and take better hold.
Hee, (quoth shee), *that will be angry without cause
Must be at one, without amendes,* by sage sawes.
Tread a woorme on the tayle, and it must turne agayne.[20]
He taketh pepper in the nose,[21] that I complayne
Upon his faultes, myselfe being faultlesse,
But that shall not stoppe my mouth yee may well gesse.
Well, (quoth I), too much of one thing is not good ;

---

[19] *Turne the leafe.*

He turneth over a new leafe and seekes by sinister meanes to effect that which otherwyse he could not by any good meanes bring to passe.—*A Health to the Gentlemanly Profession of Servingmen,* 1598.

[20] *Tread a woorme, &c.*

> The smallest worm will turn, being trodden on ;
> And doves will peck in safe-guard of their brood.
> > *3 Henry VI.* ii. 2.

[21] *He taketh pepper in the nose.*

A common expression applied to any one who was quick at taking offence.

> For every man takes pepper i' the nose
> For the wagginge of a strawe, God knowse,
> With every waverynge wynd that blowese.
> > ELDERTON'S *Lenton Stuffe,* 1570.

Leave off this ! Be it, (quoth he), fall wee to our food.
But *sufferance is no quittans* in this daiment.
No, (quoth she), nor *misreckning is no payment.*
But *even reckoning maketh long frendes ;* my frend.
For alway owne is owne, at the recknings end.
This reckning once reckned, and dinner once doone,
We three from them twaine, departed very soone.

CHAPTER V.

THIS old woman, the next day after this night,
Stale home to mee, secretly as shee might,
To talke with mee.   In secret counsell, (she
sayd),
Of things which in no wise might be bewrayd.
We twayne are one to many, (quoth I), for men say,
Three may keepe counsayle, if two be away.[22]

---

[22] *Three may keepe counsayle, &c.*

Three may keep a counsel if twain be away.
                    CHAUCER, *Ten Commandments of Love.*

Aaron. But, say again, how many saw the child ?
Nurse. Cornelia the midwife, and myself :
And no one else, but the deliver'd empress.
Aaron. The empress, the midwife, and yourself :
Two may k eep counsel, when the third's away.
                    Titus Andronicus, iv. 2.

But all that yee speake, unmeet agayne to tell,
I will say nought but mum, and *mum is counsell.*
Well then, (quoth she), herein avoyding all feares,
Avoyde your children ; *small pitchers have wyde eares.*[1]
Which done, (shee sayd), I have a husband yee know,
Whom I made of nought, as thing selfe doth show.
And for these two causes onely him I tooke,
First, that for any love he should lovingly looke,
In all kind of cause that love ingender might,
To love and cherish me by day and by night.
Secondly, the full substance which I to him brought,
He rather should augment, then bring to nought.
But now my good shall both be spent, yee shall see,
And in spending it sole instrument shall bee
Of my destruction, by spending it on such
As shall make him destroy me : I feare this much.
Hee maketh havocke, and *setteth cocke on the hoope.*
He is so lavish, the stocke beginnes to droope.
And as for gaine is dead and layd in tumbe,
When he would get ought ech finger is a thumbe.
Ech of his joyntes against other justles,

---

[1] *Small pitchers have wyde eares.*

Q. Elizabeth. A parlous boy : go to, you are too shrewd.
Archbishop. Good madam, be not angry with the child.
Q. Elizabeth. Pitchers have ears.
                                   Richard III. ii. 4.

I

As handsomly *as a beare picketh muscles.*

Flattring knaves and flering queanes being the marke,

Hang on his sleeve ; *many hands make light warke.*[2]

He hath his haukes in the mew ; but make ye sure,

With empty hands men may no haukes allure.

There is a nest of chickens, which he doth brood,

That will sure *make his hayre growe through his hood.*[3]

They can currifavell, and make fayre weather,

While they *cut large thongs of other mens leather.*[4]

He maketh his marts with marchaunts likely

To bring a shilling to nine pence quickly.

If he holds on a while as he beginnes,

We shall see him prove a marchant of eele skinnes ;

---

[2] *Many hands make light warke.*

The werke is the soner done that hathe many handes :
Many handys make light werke : my leve child.
                    How the Goode Wif Thaught hir Doughter.

[3] *Make his hayre growe through his hood.*

It wyll make hys haere growe through his hood.—*The Dis-
obedient Child,* by THOMAS INGELAND, circa 1550.

The proverb was still in use a century afterwards, being
alluded to in Middleton's comedy, *Any Thing for a Quiet Life,*
where Mistress Water-Camlet thus exclaims against a supposed
rival :—

French hood, French hood, I will make your hair grow
thorough.

[4] *Cut large thongs of other mens leather.*

                    D'autrui cuir font large curoie.
        C'est li Mariages des Filles au Dyable, MS. circa 1300.

A marchant without either money or ware.
But all bee bugs woordes, that I speake to spare.
Better spare at brim than at bottom, say I.
Ever spare, and ever bare, (saith he) ; saith th' old ballet.
What sendeth hee (say I), a staffe and a wallet.
Than up goeth his staffe to send mee aloofe ;
He is at three woordes up in the house roofe.
And herein to grow, (quoth shee), to conclusion,
I pray your ayd, to avoyde this confusion.
And for counsayle herein, I thought to have gon
To that cunning man, our curate sir John.
But this kept mee backe: I have heard now and then,
The greatest Clerkes be not the wisest men.[5]
I thinke, (quoth I), who ever that terme began,
Was neither great Clerke nor the greatest wise man.
In your running from him to me, yee runne
Out of Gods blessing into the warme Sunne.[6]

---

[5] *The greatest Clerkes be not the wisest men.*

Now I here wel, it is treue that I long syth have redde and herde, that the best clerkes ben not the wysest men.—*Historye of Reynard the Foxe,* 1481.

> The greatest clerks ben not the wisest men
> As whilom to the wolf this spake the mare.
> > CHAUCER, *Miller's Tale.*

[6] *Out of Gods blessing into the warme Sunne.*

Therefore if thou wilt follow my advice, and prosecute thine

Where the blinde leadeth the blinde, both fall in the dyke ; [7]
And blynde bee wee both, if wee thinke us his lyke.
Folkes shew much folly, when thinges should be sped,
To run to the foote, that may goe to the head.[8]
Since he best can and most ought to doo it,
I feare not but hee will, if yee will woo it.
There is but one let, (quoth she), more than I speake on :
Folke say of old ; *the shooe will hold with the sole.*
Shall I trust him then ? nay, *in trust is treason.*
But I trust you, and come to you this season,
To heare me, and tell me what way yee think best
To hem in my husband, and set me at rest.
If yee mynd, (quoth I), a conquest to make

---

own determination, thou shalt come out of a warme Sunne into
Gods blessing.—LYLY's *Euphues,* 1579.

Thou forsakest God's blessing to sit in warme Sunne.—*Ibid.*

Kent. Good king that must approve the common saw,
Thou out of heaven's benediction comest
To the warm sun.—*King Lear,* ii. 2.

[7] *Where the blinde leadeth the blinde, &c.*

> She hath hem in such wise daunted,
> That they were, as who saith, enchaunted ;
> And as the blinde an other ledeth,
> And till they falle nothing dredeth.
>
> GOWER's *Confessio Amantis.*

[8] *To run to the foote, &c.*

> Thou that stondys so sure on sete,
> Ware lest thy hede falle to thy fete.
>
> *The Boke of Curtasye,* MS. circa 1350.

Over your husband, no man may undertake
To bring you to ease or the matter amend,
Except yee bring him to weare a cocks combe at end.
For take that your husband were as yee take him,
As I take him not, as your tale would make him :
Yet were contention lyke to do nought in this,
But kepe him nought, and make him worse than he is.
But in this complaynt for counsaill quicke and cleare,
A fewe proverbes for principles, let us heare.
Who that may not as they would, will as they may ;
And this to this ; *they that are bound must obay.*
Folly is to spurne agaynst a prick ;
To strive against the streame, to winch or kicke
Against the hard wall.   By this yee may see,
Being bound to obedience, as yee bee,
And also overmatcht, suffraunce is your daunce.
Hee may overmatch me, (quoth shee), perchaunce
In strength of body, but my tongue is a limme,
To match and to vexe every vayne of him.
Tongue breaketh bone, it selfe having none,[9] (quoth I).

---

[9] *Tongue breaketh bone, &c.*

> Thou Cornysshe, quod the Hauke, by thy wil,
> Say well, or holde thee styll,
> Thou hast harde of many a man,
> Tonge breaketh bone, and it selfe hath none.
>> *Parlament of Byrdes,* circa 1550.

If the winde stand in that dore, it standeth awry.[10]

The perill of prating out of tune by note,

Telth us that a good bestill is worth a groate.

In being your owne foe you spin a fayre threede ;

Advise yee well, for here doth all lye and bleede.

Flee th' attempting of extremities all.

Folke say ; *better sit still than ryse and fall.*[11]

For little more or lesse no debate make,

At every dogs barke, seeme not to awake.

And where the small with the great can not agree,

The weaker goeth to the pot,[12] we all day see.

> "Tonge breketh bon,
>   Ant nad hire selve non,"
>   Quoth Hendyng.
>   *Proverbs of Hendyng*, MS. circa 1320.

[10] *If the winde stand in that dore.*

> *Dalio.* It is even so ? is the winde in that doore ?
>   *Supposes*, by GEORGE GASCOIGNE, 1566.

[11] *Better sit still than ryse and fall.*

Oh Cousin, I have heard my father say, that it is better to sit fast than to rise and fall, and a great wise man who knew the world to a hayre, would say, that the meane was sure : better be in the middle roome, then either in the Garret or the Sellor.— *Court and Country*, by NICHOLAS BRERETON, 1618.

[12] *The weaker goeth to the pot.*

This vulgar and objectionable saying has at least a descent from antiquity to recommend it. Judging from the context in those passages of mediæval literature where it occurs, it has been supposed to refer primarily to the barbarous practice of consigning useless or refractory monks to a species of oubliette, where in many cases they suffered a speedy death, or at the

So that alway *the bigger eateth the beane.*[13]

Yee can nought winne by any wayward meane.

Where the hedge is lowest, men may soonest over.[14]

Be silent.   Let not your tong run at rover.

Since by stryfe yee may lose, and can not winne,

Suffer!   *It is good sleeping in a whole skinne.*

If he chyde, keepe you bill under wing muet;

Chatting to chiding is *not worth a chuet.*

We see many tymes, *might overcomth right.*

Were not you *as good then to say, the crow is whight.*

And so rather let *fayre woordes make fooles fayne,*[15]

---

caprice of their superiors were permitted to linger on in life-long captivity.

The most direct allusion to these practices is in *Piers Plowman's Crede.*

> Under a pot he shall be put
> In a pryve chambre
> That he shal lyven ne laste
> But lytel whyle after.

[13] *The bigger eateth the beane.*

> For I am wery of this renning about,
> And yet alway I stand in great doubt
> Least that the bigger wyll eate the Been.
> *XII Mery Jests of the Wyddow Edyth,* 1525.

[14] *Where the hedge is lowest, &c.*

> Where hedge is lowe, there every man treads downe,
> And friendship failes, when Fortune list to frowne.
> GASCOIGNE'S *Posies,* 1575.

[15] *Fayre woordes make fooles fayne.*

In youthfull yeares, when first my yonge desires beganne
To pricke me forth to serve in court, a selender, tall yonge manne :

Then be plain without pleats, and plant your own pain.

For were yee *as playne as Dunstable hie way,*

Yet should yee that way rather breake a love day,

Than make one thus : though ye perfectly knew

All that yee conjecture to be proved true.

Yet better dissemble it, and shake it off,

Then to braide him with it in earnest or in scoffe,

If hee play faleshoode in felowship, play yee

See me and see me not ; the worst part to flee.

Why thinke yee mee so whyte liverd, (quoth shee),

That I will be tong tyed ? Well, (quoth I), your part

Is to suffer, (I say), for yee shall preeve,

Tauntes appease not thinges, they rather agreeve.

But for ill company or expense extreeme,

I heare no man doubt, so far as yee deeme ;

And there is *no fire without some smoke,* wee see.

Well, well, *make no fyre, raise no smoke,* (sayd shee).

What *cloke for the rayne*[16] so ever yee bring mee,

My fathers blessinge then I asked uppon my knee,
Who, blessinge me wyth tremblinge hand, these woordes gan say
      to me :
My sonne, God guide thy way, and shielde thee from mischaunce,
And make thy just desartes in court, thy pore estate to advaunce :
But when thou art become one of that courtlie trayne,
Thinke on this proverbe olde, quod he, that faire woordes make
      fools faine.—*Paradyse of Dayntie Devises,* 1578.

   [16] *Cloke for the rayne.*

   Nicholas. 'Tis good to have a cloake for the raine ; a bad shift

Myselfe can tell best where my shooe doth wring mee.[17]

But as yee say ; where fyre is, smoke will appeere.

And so hath it done, for I did lately heere,

How fleck and his make use their secret haunting,

By one byrd, that in myne eare was late chaunting.

One swallow maketh not summer,[18] (sayd I), men say :

I have, (quoth she), moe blocks in his way to lay,

For farther increase of suspicion of ils.

Besyde the jetting into the towne, to his Gils,

With calets hee consumeth himselfe and the goods ;

Sometyme in the fieldes, sometyme in the woods,

Some heare and see him, whom he heareth and seeth
    not,

But *fieldes have eies and woods have eares,*[19] yee wot.

---

is better then none at all ; Ile sit heere, as if I were as dead as
a doore naile.—*Two Angry Women of Abingdon,* 1599.

[17] *Myselfe can tell best where my shooe doth wring mee.*

    Je scay mieux où le bas me blesse.
                Maistre Pierre Patelin.

[18] *One swallow maketh not summer.*

One swallowe prouveth not that summer is neare.
      NORTHBROOKE'S *Treatise against Dauncing,* 1577.

[19] *Fieldes have eies and woods have eares.*

    The were bettur be still ;
    Wode has erys, felde has sijt
    Were the forster here now right,
    Thy wordis shuld like the ille.
  King Edward and the Shepherd, MS. circa 1300.

And also on my maydes he is ever tooting.

Can yee judge a man, (quoth I), by this looking?

What, *a cat may looke on a King*, yee know.

My cats leering looke, (quoth she), at first show,

Shewth me, that my cat goeth a catter wawing;

And specially by his manner of drawing

To Madge my fayre mayde; for may he come ny her,

Hee must needes basse her, as he comth by her.

He loveth well sheeps flesh, that wets his bred in the
        wull,[20]

If he leave it not, *we have a crow to pull.*[1]

---

[20] *He loveth well sheeps flesh, that wets his bred in the wull.*

The proverb must be taken to refer to a certain broth or jelly
made from the sheep's head boiled with the wool.   Such a receipt
is mentioned in a rare poem attributed to Lydgate, where the
virtues of a sheep are found enumerated :—

> Of the shepe is caste awaye no thynge;
> His horne for nockes, to haftes go his bone,
> To londe grete prouffyte dooth his tyrtelynge;
> His talowe serveth for playsters many one;
> For harpe strynges his ropes serve echone.
> Of whoos hede boyled, with wull and all,
> Tere cometh a gely and an oyntement ryal.
> > *Treatyse of the Horse, the Shepe and the goos.*

[1] *We have a crow to pull.*

> *Abelle.* Dere brother, I will fayre
> On feld ther our bestes ar,
> To looke if they be holgh or fulle.
> > *Cayn.* Na, na, abide, we have a craw to pulle.
> > > *Mactacio Abel*, in *Towneley Mysteries*, circa 1420.

He loveth her better at the sole of the foote,
Than ever hee loved mee at the hart roote.
It is a foule byrd that fyleth his owne nest.[2]
I would have him live as Gods law hath exprest,
And leave lewd ticking.   Hee that will none ill doo,
Must do nothing that belongeth theretoo ;
To ticke and laugh with me, hee hath lawfull leeve :
To that I sayd nought, but *laught in my sleeve.*
But when shee seemed to bee fixed in mynde,
Rather to seeke for that shee was loth to finde,
Than leave that seeking, by which she might find ease,
I faynde this fancy to feele how it should please.
Will yee do well, (quoth I)? take paine to watch him :

---

[2] *A foule byrd that fyleth his owne nest.*

> þu art loþlich and unclene
> Bi þine neste ich hit mene
> And ek bi þine fule brode
> þu fedest on heom a þel ful fode,
> þel þostu þat hi doþ þar inne
> Hi fuleþ hit up to þe chinne
> Heo sitteþ þar so li beo bisne
> Dahet habba þat ilke best
> þat fuleþ his oȝe nest.
>
> > *Owl and the Nightingale,* MS. circa 1250.
>
> Rede and lerne ye may,
> Howe olde proverbys say,
> That byrd ys nat honest,
> That fylyth hys owne nest.
> > SKELTON, *Poems against Garnesche,* 1520.

And if yee chaunce in advoutry to catch him,

Then *have yee him on the hip,*[3] or on the hirdell,

Then have yee his head fast under your girdell.

Where your woordes now do but *rub him on the gall,*

That deede without woordes shall drive him to the wall.

And *further than the wall he can not go:*

But must submit himselfe, and it hap so,

That at ende of your watch yee giltlesse appeere,

Then all grudge grown by jelousy, taketh end cleere.

For of all folkes I may woorst watch him (sayd shee),

Of all folkes himselfe most watcheth mee.

I shall as soone try him or take him this way,

As *dryve a top over a tyled house,* no way.

I may keepe corners or hollow trees with th'owle,

This seven yeares day and night to watch a bowle,

Before I shall catch him with undoubted evill.

Hee must have a long spoone, shall eat with the devill ;[4]

---

[3] *Have yee him on the hip.*

> Which thing to do,
> If this poor trash of Venice, whom I trash
> For his quick hunting, stand the putting on,
> I'll have our Michael Cassio on the hip.
>
> *Othello,* ii. 7.

[4] *Hee must have a long spoone, &c.*

Courtezan. Your man and you are marvellous merry, sir. Will you go with me? We'll mend our dinner here.

Dromio. Master, if you do, expect spoonmeat or bespeak a long spoon.

And the devil is no falser than is hee.

I have heard tell, it had need to bee

A wylie mouse that should breed in the cats eare.[5]

Shall I get within him than ? nay ware that geare.

It is hard halting before a creeple[6] yee wot.

A falser water drinker there liveth not.

Whan he hunteth a Doe, that he can not avow,

All dogs barke not at him, I warrant yow ;

Namely not I, (I say), though as I sayd,

Hee sometyme, though seldom, by some be bewrayed.

Close hunting, (quoth I), the good hunter allowth ;

Antipholus. Why, Dromio?

Dromio. Marry, he must have a long spoon, that must eat with the devil.—*Comedy of Errors*, iv. 3.

> Therefore behoveth him a ful long spone,
> That shal ete with a fend : thus herd I say.
>
> > CHAUCER, *Squieres Tale.*

[5] *A wylie mouse, &c.*

> A hardy mowse that is bold to breede
> In cattis eeris.—*Order of Foles*, MS. circa 1450.

> It is a wyly mouse
> That can build his dwellinge house
> Within the cattes eare.
>
> > SKELTON, 1520.

[6] *It is hard halting before a creeple.*

I perceyve (quod she) it is evill to halte before a Creple. Ferdinando, perceyving now that his Mistryse waxed angry, thought good on hir behalfe thus to answere: and it is evill to hop before them that runne for the Bell.—*Fable of Ferdinando Jeronimi and Leonora de Valases*, by GEORGE GASCOIGNE, 1575.

But bee your husband never so still of mouth,
If yee can hunt, and will stand at receite,
Your mayd examind, maketh him open streite.
That were, (quoth shee), as of my truth to make preefe,
To aske my fellow whether I be a theefe.
They *cleave together lyke burres*, that way I shall
Pyke out no more than out of the stone wall.
Than like yee not to watch him for wife or maide ?
No, (quoth shee). Nor I, (quoth he); what ever I saide
And I mislike not only your watch in vaine,
But also if yee tooke him what could yee gaine ?
From suspicion to knowledge of yll, forsooth,
Could make yee doo, but as the flounder dooth,
Leape out of the frying pan into the fyre;
And change from il paine to worse, is worth small hire.
Let time trie.   Time trieth troth in every doubt;
And deeme the best til time hath tride the troth out.
And reason saith, *make not two sorowes of one;*
But yee make ten sorowes where reason maketh none.
For where reason, (as I sayd), wilth you to winke,
(Although all were proved as ill as ye thinke),
Contrarie to reason ye stampe and ye stare;
Ye fret and ye fume *as mad as a march hare.*[7]

---

[7] *As mad as a march hare.*
    I saye, thou madde Marche hare.
SKELTON'S *Replycation against certayne yong scolers*, 1520.

Without proofe to his reproofe present or past,

But by such repoft, as most prove lyes at last.

And *here goth the hare away,*[8] for ye judge all,

And judge the worst in all, ere proofe in ought fall.

But *blind men should judge no colours,* by old sawes,

And *folke oft times are most blind in their owne cawse.*

The blinde eate many flyes.[9]   Howbeit the fancie

Of your blindnes comth not of ignorancie.

Ye could tell another herein the best way :

But *it is as folke doe, and not as folke say.*

For they say, *saying and doing are two things*

To defend danger that double dealing brings.

As ye can seeme wise in words, be wise in deede.

That is, (quoth he), *sooner sayd then done,* I dreede.

But me seemth your counsaile wayth in the whole,

To make me put my finger in a hole.

And so by suffrance to be so lither,

In my house *to lay fire and tow togither.*

---

[8] *Here goth the hare away.*
  Man. By my fayth a lytell season
I folowd the counsell and dyet of reason.
  Gets. There went the hare away.
  MEDWALL'S *Interlude of Nature,* 1510.

[9] *The blinde eate many flyes.*
      the blinde eateth many a flye :
    So doth the husband often, iwis,
    Father the childe that is not his.
      Schole-house of Women, 1541.

And if they fire me, some of them shall winne
More tow on their distaves than they can well spinne.[10]
And the best of them shall have both their hands full :
Bolster or pillow for me, be whose wul.
I will not *beare the divels sacke* by saint Audrie,
For conceiling suspition of their baudrie.
I feare false measures, or else I were a childe :
For they that thinke none ill, are soonest beguilde.
For thus though *much water goeth by the mill,*
That the miller knoweth not of,[11] yet I will
Cast what may scape, and as though I finde it,
With the clacke of my mill to fine meale grinde it.
And sure ere I take any rest in effect,
I must banish my maides such as I suspect.

---

[10] *More tow on their distaves, &c.*

In JOHN HEYWOOD'S *Merry Playe betweene the Pardoner and the Frere, the Curate and neybour Pratte,* 1533, the parson and friar having come to blows, the parson thus acknowledges his defeat :

I have more tow on my dystaffe than I can well spyn.

[11] *Much water goeth by the mill, &c.*

> *Demetrius.* Why mak'st thou it so strange ?
> She is a woman, therefore may be woo'd.
> She is a woman, therefore may be won.
> She is Lavinia, therefore must be lov'd.
> What, man ; more water glideth by the mill,
> Than wots the miller of, and easy it is
> Of a cut loaf to steal a shive.
>   *Titus Andronicus,* ii. 7.

Better it be done, than wish it had been done.

As good undone, (quoth I), as doe it too soone.

Well, (quoth she), till soone fare ye well, and this

Keepe ye as secret as ye thinke meete is.

Out at doores went she herewith : and hereupon

In at doores came he forthwith as she was gon.

And without any temprate protestation,

Thus he began in way of exclamation.

CHAPTER VI.

H what choice may compare to the divels life,

Like his that hath chosen a divell to his wife;

Namely such an old witch, such a mackabroine,

As evermore *like a hogge hangeth the groine*

On her husband, except he be her slave,

And follow all fancies that she would have.

Tis said, *there is no good accord,*

Where every man would be a Lord.

Wherefore my wife will be no Lord, but Ladie,

To make me that should be her Lord, a babie.

Before I was wedded, and since, I made reckning,

To make my wife bow at every beckning.

K

Bachelers boast, how they will teach their wives good ;
But *many a man speaketh of Robin Hood,*
That never shot in his bow. When all is sought,
Bachelers wives, and maides children be well tought.[12]
And this with this I also begin to gather,
Every man can rule a shrew, save he that hath her.
At my will I wend she should have wrought like waxe,
But I finde and feele, shee hath found such knaxe
In her bouget, and such toyes in her hed,
That *to daunce after her pipe* I am nie led.
It is said of old, *an old dog biteth sore ;*[13]
But by God, th' old bitch biteth sorer and more.
And not with teeth, (she hath none), but with her tung.
If all tales be true, (quoth I), though she be stung,
And thereby sting you, she is not much to blame,
For what ever you say, thus goeth the fame.
When folkes first saw your substance layd in your lap,
Without your paine, with your wife brought by good
     hap,
Oft in remembrance of haps happie devise,
They would say, *better be happie then wise.*

---

[12] *Bachelers wives, &c.*
The maid's child is ever best taught.—LATIMER'S *5th Sermon.*
[13] *An old dog biteth sore.*
        Olde dogges bite sore.
   CHURCHYARD'S *Handeful of Gladsome Verses,* 1592.

Not minding thereby than to deprave your wit,
For they had good hope to see good proofe of it.
But since their good opinion therein so cooles
That they say as oft, *God sendeth fortune to fooles.*
In that as fortune without your wit gave it,
So can your wit not keepe it when ye have it.
Saith one, *this geare was gotten on a holy day.*
Saith another, *who may hold that will away.*
This game from beginning shewth what end is ment;
Soone gotten soone spent, ill gotten ill spent.
Ye are calde not only too great a spender,
Too franke a giver and as free a lender:
But also ye spend, give and lend, among such,
Whose lightnes minisheth your honestie much,
As your money, and much they disalow,
That ye brake all from her, that brought all to yow,
And spend it out at doores in spite of her,
Because ye would kill her to be quite of her.
For all kindnes, of her part, that may rise,
Ye shew all th' unkindnes ye can devise.
And where reason and custome, (they say), affoords,
Alway to let the losers have their words,
Ye make her a coockqueane, and consume her good,
And she must sit *like a beane in a Munks hood.*
She must obey those lambes, or els a lambs skin
Ye will provide for her, to lap her in.

This *biteth the mare by the thumbe,* as they say.
For were ye, touching condition, (say they),
The castell of honestie in all things els,
Yet should this one thing, as their whole tale tels,
Defoyle and deface that castell to a cottage.
With many conditions good, one that is ill,
Defaceth the flowre of all and doth all spill.
Now, (quoth I), if you thinke they truly clatter,
Let your amendment amend the matter.
Halfe warnd halfe armd.   This warning for this I show,
He that hath an ill name is half hangd, ye know.

CHAPTER VII.

WELL sayd (sayd he) mary sir here is a tale ;
For honestie, *meete to set the divell on sale.*
But now am I forst a beadrole t'unfolde,
To tell somewhat more to the tale I erst tolde.
Grow this, as most part doth, I durst holde my life,
Of the jelousie of dame Julok, my wife,
Then shall ye wonder when trueth doth define,
How she can, and doth here both bite and whine.
Franzie, heresie, and jelousie are three,
That men say hardly or never cured bee.

And although jelousie need not or boot not,

What helpeth that counsaile, if reason roote not?

And in mad jelousie she is so farre gon,

She thinkth I run over all that I looke on.

Take good heede of that, (quoth I), for at a word,

The proverbe saith *he that striketh with the sword*

Shall be stricken with the scabberd.[14] Tush, (quoth he);

The divell with the scabberd will not strike me.

But my dame taking suspition for full preefe,

Reporteth it for a troth to the most mischeefe,

In words gold and hole, as men by wit could wish,

She will *as fast as a dog will lick a dish.*

She is of troth *as false as God is trew.*

And if she chance to see me at a vew

Kisse any of my maides alone, but in sport,

That takth she in earnest, *after Bedlam sort.*[15]

The cow is wood. *Her tongue runth on pattens.*

If it be morne, we have a payre of mattens;

---

[14] *He that striketh with the sword, &c.*

Nich. Blessed be the peace-makers; they that strike with the sword shall be beaten with the scabberd.

Phil. Well said, proverbs, nere another to that purpose?

Nich. Yes, I could have said to you, syr Take heede is a good reede. *Two Angry Women of Abington,* 1599.

[15] *After Bedlam sort.*

Here is an allusion to the Priory of St. Mary of Bethlehem, which was converted into an asylum in 1546, the year of the publication of Heywood's Dialogue.

If it even, evensong, not Latine nor Greeke,

But English and like that as in Easter weeke.

She beginneth first with a Cry a leysone,

To which she ringth a peale, alarum : such an one,

As folk *ring bees with basons ; the world runth on
    wheeles.*

But except her mayd *shew a fayre payre of heeles,*[16]

She haleth her by the boy rope till her braines ake.

And bring I home a good dish, good cheere to make,

What is this (saith she) ? Good meate, (say I), for yow.

God have mercie horse,[17] *a pig of mine owne sow.*

Thus when I see by kindnes ease reneweth not,

---

[16] *Shew a fayre payre of heeles.*

Prince Henry. But, Francis, darest thou be so valiant as to
play the coward with thy indenture and show it a fair pair of
heels.—1 *Henry IV.* ii. 4.

[17] *God have mercie horse.*

According to *Tarlton's Jests*, 1611, this form of speech arose
from an adventure of Richard Tarleton, the player, with Banks's
performing horse, Morocco.

The[re] was one Banks, in the time of Tarlton, who served
the Erle of Essex, and had a horse of strange qualities, and
being at the Crosse-keyes, in Gracious streete, [Gracechurch
Street] getting mony with him, as he was mightily resorted to.
Tarlton then, with his fellowes, playing at the Bel [the Red Bull
in Bishopsgate Street] by, came into the Crosse-keyes, amongst
many people, to see fashions, which Banks perceiving, to make
the people laugh, saies ; seignior, to his horse, go fetch me the
veryest foole in the company. The jade comes immediately,
and with his mouth drawes Tarlton forth. Tarlton with merry
words, said nothing but, "God a mercy, horse." In the end
Tarlton, seeing the people laugh so, was angry inwardly, and

And *that the eye seeth not, the hart reweth not ;* [18]

And that *he must needes goe whom the divell doth drive,*[19]

He forcing me for mine ease to contrive,

To let her fast and freat alone for me,

I goe where merry chat and good cheere may be.

Much spend I abroad, which at home should be spent,

If she would leave controlling and bee content.

There lept a whiting, (quoth she), and lept in streite.

Take a haire from his beard, and marke this conceite,

---

said : Sir, had I power of your horse as you have, I would doe more than that. What ere it be, said Banks, to please him, I will charge him to do it. Then, said Tarleton : charge him to bring me the veriest whore-master in the company. The horse leades his master to him. Then " God a mercy horse indeed," saies Tarlton. The people had much ado to keep peace ; but Banks and Tarlton had like to have squar'd, and the horse by to give aime. But ever after it was a by word thorow London, God a mercy horse ! and is so to this day.

[18] *That the eye seeth not, &c.*

Thou art now, Francesco, to be a lover, not a divine ; to measure thy affections by Ovid's principles, not by rules of theology. . . . . What ! the blinde eats many a flie, and much water runnes by the mill that the miller never knowes of : the evill that the eye sees not, the hart rues not. *Caste si non caute.* Tush, Francesco, Isabel hath not Lynceus eyes to see so farre. Therefore while thou art resident in London, enjoy the beauty of Infida, and when thou art at home, onely content thee with Isabel.—GREENE'S *Never too Late,* 1590.

[19] *He must needes goe, &c.*

There is a proverb which trewe now preveth,
He must nedes go that the dyvell dryveth.
HEYWOOD'S *Johan Johan the Husbande, Tyb
his wyfe and Syr Jhan the Preest,* 1533.

He maketh you beleeve, by lyes layd on by lode,
My brauling at home maketh him banquet abrode.
Where his banquets abroad, make me braule at home.
For as in a frost, a mud wall made of lome
Cracketh and crummeth in peeces asunder,
So melteth his money to the worlds wonder.
Thus may ye see *to turne the cat in the pan,*[20]
Or *set the cart before the horse*[1] well he can.
He is but little at home, the truth is so,
And forth with him he will not let me go.

---

[20] *To turne the cat in the pan.*

It may safely be maintained that the proverb as originally
spoken was, "to turn the cate in the pan ;" *cate* being an old
word for *cake.*

> Feasting with Pluto and his Proserpine .
> Night after night with all delicious cates.
> > *The Hog hath lost his Pearl.*

It is supposed that *cate* takes its origin from the final syllable
of the word *delicate;* and that from this comes our modern
word to *cater.*

Some philologers have seen in this phrase a corruption of
the French *guet-a-pens,* and others refer it to the Low Latin
catapanus, or the Greek καταπαύω.

As for Bernard, often tyme he turneth the cat in the pan.
> SHACKLOCK'S *Hatchet of Heresies,* 1565.

[1] *Set the cart before the horse.*

> Il mettoyt la charette devant les beufz.
> > RABELAIS.

This is Harry White's humour.

Item. He deemes that a preposterous government where the
wife predominates, and the husband submits to her discretion,
that is Hysterion and Proteron, the cart before the horse.
> *Harry White, his Humour.*

And if I come to be merry where he is,

Then is he mad, as ye shall heare by this.

Where he with gossips at a banquet late was,

At which as use is, he payd all, but let pas :

I came to be merrie.   Wherewith merrily,

Proface.   *Have among you, blinde harpers,*[2] (say'd I) ;

The moe the merrier,[3] we all day here see.

Yea, but *the fewer the better fare,* (sayd he).

Then here were, ere I came, (quoth I), too many ;

Here is but little meate left, if there be any.

And *it is ill comming,* I have heard say,

---

[2] *Have among you, blinde harpers.*

Macaulay observes that in the old ballad poetry, all the gold is " red " and all the ladies " gay."   So also, it may be remarked that, as in the instance before us, all the harpers are afflicted with blindness.   The " have among you " is merely an expression of conviviality accompanying the drinking of a toast.

> *Leoc.* Have towards thee, Philotas.
> *Phil.* To thee, Archippus.
> *Arch.* To thee, Molops.
> *Molops.* Have among you, blind fiddlers.
>   CARTWRIGHT'S *Royall Slave,* 1651.

" The Poet's Blind Man's Bough : or Have among you blinde Harpers " was the title of a tract by Martin Parker, printed in 1651.

[3] *The moe the merrier.*

> Store makes no sore : loe this seemes contrarye,
> And mo the merier is a Proverbe eke,
> But store of sores maye make a maladye,
> And one to many maketh some to seeke,
> When two be mette that bankette with a leche.
>   GASCOIGNE'S *Posies,* 1575.

To th' end of a shot, and beginning of a fray.
Put by thy purse, (quoth he), thou shalt not pay.
And fray here should be none, were thou gone thy way.
Here is since thou camst *too many feete a bed.*
Welcome when thou goest ; thus is thine errand sped.
I come, (quoth I), to be one here, if I shall,
It is merrie in hall when beards wagge all.[4]
What, bid me welcome pig : I pray thee kisse me :
Nay farewell sow, (quoth he), our Lord blesse me
From *bassing of beasts of Bearebinder lane.*
I have, (quoth I), for fine sugar, fayre rats bane.
Many yeares since my mother sayd to me,
Her elders would say, *it is better to be*
An old mans derling than a yong mans werling.
In my old husbands daies, for as tenderly
He loved me as ye love me slenderly,
We drew both in one line.   Quoth he, would to our Lord
Ye had, in that drawing *hangd both in one cord.*
For I never meete thee at flesh nor at fish,

---

[4] *It is merrie in hall when beards wagge all.*
     Swithe mury hit is in halle,
     When burdes wawen alle.
                              Life of Alexander, 1312.

  Silence. Be merry, be merry, my wife has all ;
     For women are shrews, both short and tall,
     'Tis merry in hall, when beards wag all.
                              2 *Henry IV.* v. 3.

But I have sure *a dead mans head in my dish.*[5]
Whose best and worst day, that wisht may be,
Was when thou didst burie him and marrie me.
If you, quoth I, long for change in these cases,
Would to God he and you had changed places.
But best I change place, for here I may be sparde,
And for my kinde comming, this is my rewarde.
Must she not, (quoth he), be welcome to us all,
Among us all letting such a farewell fall ?
Such carpenters, such chips, (quoth she), folke tell,
Such lips, such lettice, such welcome, such farewell.
Thine owne words, (quoth he), thine owne welcome
      mard.
Well, (said she), whensoever we twaine have jard,
My words be pried at narrowly I espie,
Ye can see a mote in another mans eie,
But ye cannot see a balke in your owne.
Ye marke my wordes, but not that they be growne
By your revellous riding on every royle,[6]
Welny every day a new mare or a moyle,
As much unhonest as unprofitable,
Which shall bring us shortly to be unable,

---

[5] *A dead mans head in my dish.*
  As bold-fac'd women, when they wed another;
  Banquet their husbands with their dead love's heads.
             MARSTON'S *Insatiate Countess.*
[6] *Royle, i.e.* a Flemish horse.

To give a dog a loafe, as I have oft said.

How be it your pleasure may no time be denaid,

But still you must have both the finest meate,

Apparell, and all things that money may get,

Like one of fond fancie so fine and so neate,

That *would have better bread than is made of wheate.*

The best is best cheape,[1] (quoth he), men say cleere.

Well, (quoth she), *a man may buy gold too deere.*

Ye neither care, nor welny cast what ye pay,

To buy the deerest for the best alway.

Then for your diet who useth feeding such,

Eate more than enough, and drinke much more too
        much.

But temprance teacheth this, where he keepeth
        schoole ;

He that knoweth when he hath enough is no foole.

Feed by measure, and defie the phisition !

And in the contrarie mark this condition ;

A swine over fat is cause of his owne bane.

Who seeth nought herein, his wit is in the wane.

But pompous provision, comth not all alway

---

[1] *The best is best cheape.*

> Whereto shuld I threpe ?
> With my staff can I lepe,
> And men say, " lyght chepe
>   Letherly for-yeldys."
>
> *Towneley Mysteries,* circa 1420.

Of gluttonie, but pride sometime, some say.

But this proverbe preacheth to men haute or hie,

Hew not too hie, lest the chips fall in thine eye.[8]

Measure is a merrie meane,[9] as this doth show,

Not too hie for the pie nor too low for the crow.

The difference between staring and stark blinde,

The wise man at all times to follow can finde.

And ywis an auditour of a meane wit,

May soone account, though hereafter come not yit.

Yet is he sure *be the day never so long,*

Evermore at last they ring to evensong.[10]

And where ye spend much though ye spent but lickell,

Yet *little and little the cat eateth the flickell.*

Little losse by length may grow importable.

A mouse in time may bite a two a cable.

Thus to end of all things, be we leefe or loth,

---

[8] *Hew not too hie, &c.*

For an old proverbe it is ledged " he that heweth to hie, with chips he may lose his sight." CHAUCER, *Testament of Love.*

[9] *Measure is a merrie meane.*

  Magn. Yet mesure is a mery mene.
  Fan. Ye, syr, a blannched almonde is no bene,
  Measure is mete for a marchauntes hall.
     Interlude of Magnyfycence, circa 1520.

[10] *Be the day never so long, &c.*

  For though the day be never so long
  At last the bell rings for evensong.
     STEPHEN HAWES, *Pastime of Pleasure.*

Yet loe, *the pot so long to the water goth,*
Till at last it commeth home broken.[11]
Few words to the wise suffise to be spoken.
If ye were wise, here were enough, (quoth she).
Here is enough and too much, dame, (quoth he).
For though this appeare a proper pulpit peece,
Yet *when the foxe preacheth, then beware your geese.*
A good tale ill tolde, in the telling is mard.
So are, (quoth she), good tales well tolde, and ill hard.
Thy tales, (quoth he), shew *long haire and short wit,*[12]
  wife.

---

[11] *The pot so long to the water goth, &c.*

And therfore it is a trew proverbe, þat " The potte may goo
so longe to water, that atte the laste it is broken ;" as this leude
woman that had her husbonde ten tymes fairer thanne the
prioure the which she toke, and that she was ascaped bi the
helpe of the false bauude her godsib of ij suche periles that her
husbonde hadde founde by her, and after that she had broken
her husbondes comaundement, and therefor he brake her legges,
and yet she wolde not be chastised.—*The Book of the Knight
of La Tour-Landry*, MS. circa 1450.

As every storme hath his calme, and the greatest spring-tide
the deadest ebbe, so fared it with Francesco ; for so long went
the pot to the water, that at last it came broken home, and so long
put he his hand into his purse, that at last the empty bottome
returned him a writ of *Non est inventus :* for well might the divell
daunce there, for ever a crosse there was to keep him backe.—
GREENE'S *Never too Late,* 1590.

[12] *Long haire and short wit.*

  Hair ! 'tis the basest stubble ; in scorn of it
  The proverb sprung,—He has more hair than wit.
     DECKER'S *Satiromastix,* 1602.

But *long be thy legs, and short be thy life.*
Pray for yourself. I am not sick, (quoth she).
Well lets see what thy last tale comth to, (quoth he).
Thou saist I spend all, to this thy words wander :
But *as deepe drinketh the goose as the gander.*
Thou canst cough in the aumbrie if neede bee,
When I shall cough without bread or broth for thee.
Whereby while thou sendst me abrode to spend,
Thou gossipst at home *to meete me at lands end.*
Well, thou wouldst have me, (quoth he), pinch like a
      snudge.
Every day to be thy drivell and drudge.
Not so, (quoth she), but I would have ye sturre
Honestly *to keepe the woolfe from the durre.*
I would drive the woolfe out of doore first, (quoth he) ;
And that can I not doe, till I drive out thee.
A man were better be drownd in Venice gulfe
Than have such a bearded beare, or such a woolfe.
But had I not been witcht, my wedding to flee,
The termes that long to wedding had warnd mee,
First wooing for woing, banna for banning,
The banes for my bane, and then this thus scanning.

Speed. Item she hath more hair than wit.
Launce. More hair than wit,—it may be ; I'll prove it : The
cover of the salt hides the salt, and therefore it is more than the
salt : the hair, that covers the wit, is more than the wit, for the
greater hides the less.—*Two Gentlemen of Verona,* iii. 2.

Marrying, marring. And what maried I than ?
A woman. As who say, woe to the man.
Thus wed I with woe, wed I Gill, wed I Jane,
I pray God the divell goe with thee downe the lane.
I graunt, (quoth she), this doth sound, (as ye agreed),
On your side in words, but on my side in deede.
Thou grantst this graunt, (quoth he), without any grace
Ungraciously, to thy side to turne this case.
Leave this, (quoth she), and leave liberalitie,
To stint strife, growne by your prodigalitie.
Oft said the wise man, whom I erst did berrie,
Better are meales many, than one too merrie.
Well, (quoth he), that is answered with this, wife :
Better is one months cheere, than a churles whole life.
I thinke it learning of a wiser lectour,
To learne to make my selfe mine owne erectour,
Than spare for another that might wed thee,
As the foole thy first husband spared for mee.
And as for ill places, thou seekest me in more
And in woorse too, than I into any goe.
Whereby this proverbe shewth thee in by the weeke,
No man will another in the oven seeke,
Except that himselfe hath been there before.[13]

---

[13] *No man will another in the oven seeke, except that himselfe hath been there before.*

A hackney proverb in mens mouths ever since King Lud was

God give grace thou hast been good, I say no more,

And would have thee say lesse except thou couldst
prove

Such processe as thou slanderously dost move.

For slaunder perchance, (quoth she), I not deny,

It may be a slaunder, but it is no ly.

It is a lye, (quoth he), and thou a lier.

Will ye, (quoth she), drive me to touch ye nyer?

I rub the gald horse back, till he winch, and yit,

He would make it seeme that I touch him no whit.

But I wot what I wot, though I few words make:

Many kisse the child for the nurses sake.

Ye have many god children to looke upon,

And ye blesse them all, but ye basse but one.

This *halfe shewth what the whole meaneth*, that I meeve,

Ye fetch circumquaques to make me beleeve,

Or thinke, that *the moone is made of a greene cheese.*[14]

And when ye have made me a lout in all these,

It seemeth ye would make me goe to bed at noone.

---

a little boy, or Belinus, Brennus' brother, for the love hee bare to
oysters, built Billingsgate.—NASH'S *Have with you to Saffron
Waldon,* 1596.

[14] *The moone is made of a greene cheese.*

Whilst they tell for truthe Luther his lowde lyes, so that they
may make theyr blinde brotherhode and the ignorant sort beleve
that the mone is made of grene chese.—SHACKLOCK'S *Hatchet of
Heresies,* 1565.

L

Nay, (quoth he), the day of doome shall be doone,
Ere thou goe to bed at noone or night for mee.
Thou art, (to be plaine and not to flatter thee),
As holsome a morsell for my comely corse
As a shoulder of mutton for a sicke horse.
The divell with his dam hath more rest in hell,
Than I have here with thee : but well, wife, well !
Well, well, (quoth she), *many wels, many buckets.*
Yea, (quoth he), and *many words, many buffets.*
Had you some husband, and snapt at him thus,
I wis he would give you a recumbentibus.
A dog will barke ere he bite, and so thow,
After thy barking wilt bite me, I trow now.
But *it is hard to make an old dog stoup,* lo.
Sir, (quoth she), a man may handle his dog so
That he may make him bite him, though he would not.
Husbands are in heaven, (quoth he), *whose wives scold*
         not.
Thou makest me *claw where it itcheth not.*   I would
Thy tongue were coold to make thy tales more cold.
That aspen leafe such spitefull clapping hath bred,
That *my cap is better at ease then my head.*
God send that head, (sayd she), a better nurse :
For when the head aketh, all the bodie is the wurse.
God grant, (quoth I), the head and bodie both two,
To nurse each other better then they do :

Or ever have done for the most times past.

I brought to nurse both, (quoth she), had it not been
　　　wast.

Margerie good cow, (quoth he), *gave a good meale :*

But then she cast it downe againe with her heele.

How can her purse for profit be delitefull,

Whose person and properties be thus spitefull?

A peece of a kid is worth two of a cat.

Who the divell will change a rabet for a rat ?

If I might change, I would rather choose to begge,

Or sit with a roasted apple or an egge,

Where mine appetite serveth mee to bee,

Then every day *to fare like a Duke* with thee.

Like a Duke, like a Duke, (quoth she), thou shalt fare,

Except thou wilt spare more than thou dost yet spare.

Thou farest too well (quoth he), but thou art so wood,

Thou knowst not who doth thee harme, who doth thee
　　　good.

Yes yes, (quoth she), for all those wise words uttred,

I know on which side my bread is buttred : [15]

But there will no butter cleave on my bread :

And on my bread any butter to be spread ;

Every promise that thou therein dost utter,

---

[15] *I know on which side my bread is buttred.*

One of the proverbs Samuel Fox has jotted down in his common-
place book, MS. LANSDOWNE, 679.

Is as sure as it were *sealed with butter*,
Or *a mouse tyed with a threed.*　Every good thing
Thou lettest even slip, like a waghalter slipstring.
But take up in time, or els I protest,
All be not in bed that shall have ill rest.
Now goe to thy derlings, and declare thy griefe :
Where all thy pleasure is, hop whore, pipe thiefe.

CHAPTER VIII.

ITH this thence hopt she, wherewith, O Lord,
　　he cride,
　　What wretch but I, this wretchedness could
　　bide ?
Howbeit in all this woe, I have no wrong,
For it onely is all on my selfe along.
Where I should have bridled her first with rough bit,
To have made her chew on the bridle one fit,
For licorous lucre of a little winning,
I gave her the bridle at beginning.
And now she taketh the bridle in the teeth,
And runn'th away with it, whereby each man seeth,
It is, (as old men right well understand),

Ill putting a nak't sword in a mad mans hand.
She takth such hart of grace,[16] though I maime her,
Or kill her, yet shall I never reclaime her.
She hath, (they say), been stiffe necked evermore,
And *it is ill healing of an old sore.*
This proverbe prophecied many yeares agone,
It will not out of the flesh, that is bred in the bone.[17]
What chance have I, to have a wife of such sort,
That will no fault amend in earnest nor sport?
A small thing amisse lately I did espie,
Which to make her mend, by a jest merrilie,
I said but this; *taunt tivet wife, your nose drops,*
So it may fall, I will eate no browesse sops
This day. But two daies after this came in ure,
I had sorow to my sops enough, be sure.
Well (quoth I), *it is ill jesting, on the sooth:*

---

[16] *She takth such hart of grace.*

This proverbial sentence would seem to have originally been "to take heart at grass" from the idea of an animal at grass becoming strong and hearty.

Seeing she would take no warning, on a day took heart at grasse, and belabour'd her well with a cudgel.—TARLTON'S *News out of Purgatory*, 1590.

[17] *It will not out of the flesh, &c.*

Downright. He values me at a crack'd three farthings, for aught I see. It will never out of the flesh that's bred in the bone. I have told him enough, one would think, if that would serve: but counsel to him is as good as a shoulder of mutton to a sick horse.—BEN JONSON, *Every Man in his Humour.*

Sooth bourd is no bourd,[18] in ought that mirth dooth.

Such jests could not juggle her, were ought amis,

Nor turne melancholy to mirth : for it is

No playing with a straw before an old cat;

Every trifling toy age cannot laugh at.

Ye may walke this way, but sure ye shall finde,

The further ye goe, the further behinde.

Ye shoulde consider the woman is olde :

And what for a hot word. *Soone hot, soone colde.*

Beare with them that beare with you, for she is scand,

Not onely the fairest flowre in your garland,

But also she is all the faire flowers thereof.

Will ye requite her then with a taunting scof,

Or with any other kinde of unkindnes ?

Take heede is a faire thing : beware this blindnes.

Why will ye, (quoth he), I shall follow her will,

To make me John drawlatch,[19] or such a snekebill,

To bring her solace that bringeth me sorow ?

---

[18] *Sooth bourd is no bourd.*

Sooth is an old English word meaning " in earnest ;" *bourd* means "a jest."

As the old saying is, sooth boord is no boord.—HARRINGTON'S *Briefe Apologie of Poetrie,* 1591.

[19] *John drawlatch.*

Well, phisition, attend me in my chamber heere, till Stilt and I returne ; and if I pepper him not, say I am not worthy to be cald a duke but a drawlatch.—*Tragedy of Hoffman,* 1602.

Bir Ladie, *then shall we catch birds to morow.*
A good wife maketh a good husband, (they say).
That (quoth I), you may turne another way:
To make a good husband, make a good wife :
I can no more herein, but God stint all strife.
Amen, (quoth he), and God have mercie brother,
I will now mend this house and payre another.
And that he ment of likelihood by his owne ;
For so appaird he that, ere three yeares were growne,
That little and little he decayed so long,
Till he at length *came to buckle and bare thong.*
To discharge charge, that necessarily grew,
There was *no more water then the ship drew.*
Money and money worth did so misse him,
That he had not now *one peny to blisse him.*
Which foreseene in this woman, wisely waying,
That meet was to stay somewhat for her staying,
To keepe yet one messe for Alison in store,
She kept one bagge, that he had not seene before.
A poore cooke that may not licke his owne fingers ; [20]
But about her at home now still he lingers,

---

[20] *A poore cooke, &c.*

He is an evyll coke y^t can not lycke his owne lippes.—*Vulgaria Stambrigi,* circa 1510.

Capulet. Sirrah, go hire me twenty cunning cooks.

2 *Servant.* You shall have none ill, sir ; for I'll try if they can lick their fingers.—*Romeo and Juliet,* iv. 2.

But whether any secret tales were sprinkling,
Or that he by gesse had *got an inkling*
Of her hoord : or that he thought to amend
And turne his ill beginning to a good end,
In shewing himselfe a new man, as was fit,
That appeared shortly after, but not yit.

CHAPTER IX.

ONE day in their arbour which stood so to
mine,
That I might and did closely mine eare incline,
And likewise cast mine eare to heare and see,
What they said and did, where they could not see mee,
He unto her a goodly tale began,
More like a wooer than a wedded man,
As far as matter thereof therein served,
But the first part from words of wooing swerved :
And stood upon repentance, with submission
Of his former crooked unkind condition.
Praying her to forgive and forget all free,
As he forgave her, as he forgiven would bee :
Loving her now as he full deeply swore,
As hotly as ever he loved her before.

Well, well, (quoth she), whatever ye now say,
It is too late to call againe yesterday.
Wife, (quoth he), such may my diligence seeme,
That th' offence of yesterday I may redeeme.
God taketh me as I am, and not as I was;
Take you me so too, and let all things past pas.
I pray thee good wife, think I speake and thinke
     plaine,
What! *he runn'th far that never turnth againe.*
Ye be yong enough to mend, I agree it,
But I am, (quoth she), too old to see it.
And amend ye or not, I am too old a yeere:
What is life, where living is extinct cleere,
Namely at old yeares of least helpe and most
     neede?
But no tale could tune you in time to take heede.
If I tune myself now, (quoth he), it is faire:
And hope of true tune, shall tune me from dispaire.
Beleeve well and have well, men say. Yea, (said shee);
Doe well and have well, men say also, we see.
But what man can beleeve, that man can doe well,
Who of no man will counsaile take, or heare tell?
Which to you, when any man any way tride,
Then were ye deafe, *ye could not heare on that side.*
Who ever with you any time therein weares,
He must *both tell you a tale, and lend you eares.*

You had on your harvest eares,[1] thicke of hearing,

But this is a question of old enquering:

Who is so deafe or so blinde, as is hee,

That wilfully will neither heare nor see?

When I saw your maner, my heart for woe molt.

Then would ye *mend as the fletcher mends his bolt,*

Or sowre ale mendeth in summer, I know,

And *knew, which way the winde blew* and will blow.

Though not to my profit a prophet was I:

I prophecied this, too true a prophecie.

When I was right ill beleeved, and worse hard,

By flinging from your folkes at home, which all mard.

When I said in semblance either cold or warme,

A man far from his good, is nigh his harme.

Or wild ye to looke, that ye lost no more,

On such, as shew that *hungrie flyes bite sore.*

Then would ye looke over me with stomack swolne,

Like as the divell look't over Lincolne.[2]

---

[1] *You had on your harvest eares.*

Thine eares be on pilgrimage, or in the wildernes, as they say commonly, thou hast on thy harvest eares, *vestræ peregrinantur aures.—Withal's Dictionary,* 1608.

[2] *Like as the divell look't over Lincolne.*

A Tour through England and Wales, 1742, gives the following as the origin of the proverb :—

The middle or Rood tower of Lincoln cathedral is the highest in the whole kingdom, and when the spire was standing on it, it must, in proportion to the height of the tower, have exceeded

The divell is dead wife, (quoth he), for ye see,

I looke like a Lambe in all your words to mee.

Looke as ye list now, (quoth she), thus look't ye than;

And for those lookes I shew this, to shew each man,

Such proofe of this proverbe, as none is greater:

Which saith, that *some man may steale a horse better*

Than some other may stand and looke upon.[3]

Lewd huswives might have words, but I not one

That might be allowd.   But now if ye looke,

In mistaking me ye may see, yee tooke

---

that of old St. Paul's, which was five hundred and twenty feet. The monks were so proud of this structure, that they would have it that the Devil looked upon it with an envious eye: whence the proverb of a man who looks invidious and malignant, " he looks as the Devil over Lincoln."

Another account is given by Ray in 1737 :—

Some refer this to Lincoln Minster, over which when first finished, the Devil is supposed to have looked with a torne and terrick countenance, as envying men's costly devotion, saith Dr. Fuller; but more probable it is, that it took its rise from a small image of the Devil, standing on the top of Lincoln College, in Oxford.

It will be remembered that in Sir Walter Scott's novel of *Kenilworth,* Giles Gosling, the host of the Black Bear at Cumnor, thus addresses Tressilian :—" Here be a set of good fellows willing to be merry ; do not scowl on them like the Devil looking over Lincoln."

[3] *Some man may steale a horse, &c.*

Tophas. Good Epi, let mee take a nap ; for as some man may better steale a horse then another looke over a hedge ; so divers shall be sleepie when they would fainest take rest.—LYLY'S *Endimion,* 1591.

The wrong way to wood, and *the wrong sow by th' eare ;*[4]
And thereby *in the wrong box to thrive,* yee were.
I have heard some to some tell this tale not seeld,
When thrift is in the towne, yee be in the feeld.
But contrary, you make that sense to sowne,
Whan thrift was in the field, ye ware in the towne.
Field ware must sinke or swim, while ye had eny :
Towne ware was your ware, to turne the peny.
But towne or field, where most thrift did appiere,
What ye wan iu the hundred, ye lost in the shiere.
In all your good husbandrie, thus rid the rock,
Ye stumbled at a straw, and lept over a block.[5]
So many kindes of increase you had in choice,
And nought increase or keepe, how can I rejoice ?
Good riding at two ankers, men have tolde,
For if the tone faile, the tother may holde.
But you leave all ankerhold on seas and lands :

---

[4] *The wrong sow by th' eare.*

Downright. Well ! he knows what to trust to, for George ;
let him spend, and spend, and domineer till his heart ake, an he
think to be relieved by me, when he has got into one o'your city
pounds, the counters, he has the wrong sow by the ear, i'faith ;
and claps his dish at the wrong man's door.—JONSON'S *Every
Man in his Humour,* ii. 7.

[5] *Ye stumbled at a straw, &c.*

This tale touchethe them, that wolde cover a smalle offence.
with a greatter wyckednesse ; and as the proverbe sayethe :
Stomble at a strawe, and leape over a blocke.—*Mery Tales and
Quicke Answeres,* 1567.

And so *set up shop upon Goodwins sands.*

But as folke have a saying both old and trew,

In that they say, *blacke will take none other hew.*

So may I say heere, to my deepe dolour,

It is a bad cloth that will take no colour.

This case is yours.   For ye were so wise,

To take specke of colour, of good advise.

Th' advise of all friends I say, one and other

Went in at the tone eare and out at the tother.[6]

And as those words went out, this proverbe in came,

He that will not be ruled by his owne dame,

Shall be ruled by his stepdame ; and so you,

Having lost your owne good, and owne friends now,

May seeke your forreine friends, if you have any.

And sure one of my great griefs, among many,

Is that ye have been so very a hog

To my friends.   What man, *love me, love my dog.*[7]

---

[6] *In at the tone eare and out at the tother.*

> But Troilus, that nigh for sorrow deide,
> Tooke little hede of all that ever he ment ;
> One eare it heard, at the other out it went.
> > CHAUCER, *Troilus and Creseide.*

[7] *Love me, love my dog.*

This was a proverb in the time of Saint Bernard :—Dicitur certe vulgari quodam proverbio : Qui me amat, amet et canem meum.—*In Festo S. Michaelis. Sermo Primus.*

Cudora. Love me ?—love my dog !

Tharsalis. I am bound to that by the proverb, madam.
> CHAPMAN'S *Widow's Tears,* 1612.

But you *to cast precious stones before hogs*
Cast my good before a sort of dogs
And sawte bitches : which by whom now devoured,
And your honestie among them defloured,
And that you may no more expence afoord,
Now can they not affoord you one good woord,
And you them as few.   And old folke understood,
When theeves fall out, true men come to their good.
Which is not alway true.   For in all that bretch,
I can no farthing of my good the more fetch,
Nor I trow themselves neither, if they were sworne.
Light come, light goe.[8]   And sure since we were borne,
Ruine of one ravine, was there none gretter :
For by your gifts they be as little the better,
As you be much the worse, and I cast away.
An ill winde that bloweth no man to good,[9] men say.
Well (quoth he), *every winde blowth not downe the corne.*
I hope, (I say), good hap be not all out-worne.
I will now begin thrift, when thrift seemeth gone.

---

[8] *Light come, light goe.*

> Wyte thou wele it schall be so,
> That lyghtly cum, schall lyghtly go.
>   *Debate of the Carpenters Tools.*

[9] *An ill winde, &c.*

Falstaff. What wind blew you hither, Pistol?
Pistol. Not the ill wind which blows no man to good.
                              2 Henry IV. v. 3.

What wife! *there be more waies to the wood than one.*

And I will assay all the waies to the wood,

Till I finde one way, to get againe this good.

Ye will get it againe, (quoth she), I feare,

As shortly as a horse will licke his eare.

Good words bring not ever of good deedes good hope,

And these words shew your words spoken in skorne,

It pricketh betimes that will be a good thorne.[10]

Timely crooketh the tree, that will a good camok bee.[11]

And *such beginning such end,* we all day see.

And you by me at beginning being thriven,

And then to keepe thrift could not be prickt nor driven.

How can ye now get thrift, the stocke being gon,

Which is the onely thing to raise thrift upon?

Men say, *he may ill runne that cannot goe,*

And your gaine without your stocke runneth even so.

For *what is a workman without his tooles?*

Tales of Robin Hood are good for fooles.

---

[10] *It pricketh betimes that will be a good thorne.*
In the interlude of *Jacob and Esau,* 1568, the old nurse Debora, while making preparations for Isaac's repast, sings :—

> It hath bene a proverbe before I was borne,
> Yong doth it pricke that wyll be a thorne.

[11] *Timely crooketh the tree, &c.*

A camok is a crooked piece or knee of timber, most frequently used in ship-building.

Timely, madam, crooks the tree that will be a camock, and young it pricks that will be a thorn.—LYLY's *Endimion.*

Hee can ill pype, that lacketh his upper lippe.

Who lacketh a stock, his gaine is not worth a chip.

A tale of a tubbe :[12] your tale no truth avouth,

Ye speake now as yee would creepe into my mouth ;

In pure paynted processe, *as false as fayre,*

How yee will amend, when ye cannot apayre.

I heard once a wise man say to his daughter,

Better is the last smile, than the first laughter.

Wee shall I trust, (quoth he), laugh again at last,

Although I be once out of the saddle cast.

Yet since I am bent to sit, this will I doo,

Recover the horse, or leese the saddle too.

---

[12] *A tale of a tubbe.*

The translator of Della Casa's *Galatea,* 1576, finds for an Italian phrase signifying " contention," the English equivalent " a tale of a tubbe."   Such, he says, it is to say :—

Such an one that was the sonne of such a one, that dwelt in Cocamer street : do you knowe him ? he married the daughter of Gianfigliazzi, the leane scragg that went so much to St. Laraunce. No, do not you know him ? why do not you remember the goodly strayght old man that ware long haire downe to his shoulders ? &c.

In BEN JONSON'S comedy of this name, when Squire Tub of Tottenham commands the company of mechanics to perform a stage play before him, he directs,—

> I'd have a toy presented,
> A Tale of a Tub, a story of myself,
> You can express a Tub ?

To which Medlay, the joiner, replies :—

> I can express a wash-house, if need be,
> With a whole pedigree of Tubs.

Yee never could yet, (quoth shee), recover any hap,
To win or save ought, to stoppe any one gap.
For stopping of gap, (quoth he), care not a rush.
I will learne *to stop two gaps with one bush.*
Yee will, (quoth shee), as soone stop gaps with rushes
As with any husbandly handsom bushes.
Your tales have lyke tast, where temprance is taster,
To *breake my head, and then geve me a plaster.*
Now thrift is gone, now would yee thrive in all haste,
And whan yee had thrift, yee had lyke hast to waste.
Yee liked then better an ynch of your will,
Than an ell of your thrift. Wife, (quoth he), be still.
May I be holpe foorth an ynch at a pinch,
I will yet thrive, (I say), *as good is an ynch*
As an ell. Yee can, (quoth shee), make it so well,
For when *I gave you an inch, you tooke an ell,*
Till both ell and inch be gone, and we in det.
Nay, (quoth he), *with a wet finger*[13] ye can set
As much as may easily all this matter ease,
And this debate also pleasantly appease.
I could doo as much with an hundred pounds now,

---

[13] *With a wet finger.*

To obtain anything with a wet finger seems to be a figurative
phrase for obtaining it with ease ; and is supposed to derive its
use from the habit of tracing a lady's name on the table with
spilt wine to serve the purposes of gallantry and intrigue. Such a
practice was not unknown to the amatory poets of antiquity :—

M

As with a thowsand afore, I assure you.

Yea, (quoth she), *who had that he hath not, would*

Doo that hee doth not, as old men have told.

Had I as yee have I would do more (quoth hee)

Than the Priest spake of on Sunday, yee should see.

Ye doo, as I have, (quoth shee), for nought I have,

And nought yee doo.   What man ! I trow yee rave.

Would yee *both eat your cake, and have your cake ?*

Yee have had of mee al that I would make ;

And bee a man never so greedy to win,

Hee can have no more of the foxe but the skin.

Well, (quoth he), if ye list to bring it out,

Yee can geve me your blessing in a cloute.

That were for my childe, (quoth she), had I ony,

Verba leges digitis, verba notata mero.

OVID, *Amor.* i. 4. 20.

So in Tibullus, lib. i. el. 6 :—

Neu te decipiat nutu, digitoque liquorem

Ne trahat, et mensæ ducat in orbe notas.

The use of this expression is frequent among the Elizabethans, but does not seem to have descended to the later writers.

Enquire what gallants sup in the next room ; and if they be any of your acquaintance, do not you, after the city fashion, send in a pottle of wine and your name, . . . but rather keep a boy in fee, who underhand shall proclaim you in every room, what a gallant fellow you are, how much you spend yearly in taverns, what a great gamester, what custom you bring to the house, in what witty discourse you maintain a table, what gentlewomen or citizens' wives you can with a wet finger have at any time to sup with you, and such like.—*The Gull's Hornbook,* 1609.

But husband, I have neither child nor mony.

Yee cast and conjecture thus much, lyke in show,

As the blind man casts his staffe, or shootes at the
* crow ;*

How be it, had I money right much, and yee none,

Yet to be plaine, yee should have for Jone.

Nay, hee that first flattreth me, as yee have doone,

And doth, as yee did to me after, so soone :

Hee may be in my Pater noster in deede,

But be sure, he shall never come into my Creede.[14]

Ave Maria, (quoth he), how much motion

Here is to prayers, with how little devotion.

But some men say, *no peny, no Pater noster.*[15]

---

[14] *Hee may be in my Pater noster, &c.*

I trust yee remember your jugling at Newington with a
christall stone, your knaveries in the wood by Wanstead, the
wondrous treasure you would discover in the Isle of Wight, al
your villanies about that peece of service, as perfectly known to
some of my friends yet living as their Pater-noster, who curse the
time you ever came into their creed.—CHETTLE'S *Kind-Heart's*
Dream, 1592.

[15] *No peny, no Pater noster.*

The Pater-noster, which was wont to fill a sheet of paper, is
written in the compasse of a penny ; whereupon one merrily
assumed that proverbe to be derived, No penny no pater-noster.
Which their nice curtayling putteth mee in minde of the custome
of the Scythians, who, if they had beene at any time distressed
with famine, tooke in their girdles shorter.—GREENE'S *Arcadia,*
1587.

I say to such, (sayd shee), *no longer foster,*
No longer lemman.   But faire and well than,
Pray and shift ech one for himselfe as hee can.
Everyman for himselfe and God for us all.
To those wordes he sayd nought, but forthwith did
        fall
From harping on that string, to faire flattring speech,
And as I erst sayd, hee did her so beseech,
That things erst so far off, were now so far on,
That as shee may wallow, away shee is gon,
Where all that was left lay with a trustie frend,
Dwelling a good walke from her at the townes end.
And backe againe straight a halting pace she
        hobles,
Bringing a bag of royals and nobles,
All that she had without restraint of one jote.
She brought bullocks noble: for noble or grote
Had she not one more: which I after well knew.
And anone smiling toward him as she drew, ·
A sir, *light burden, far heavie,* (quoth she);
This light burden in long walke welny tyreth me.
God give grace I play not the foole this day;
For here *I send th' axe after the helme away.*
But if ye will stint and avoyd all strife,
Love and cherish this, as ye would my life.
I will (quoth he), wife, by God almightie,   .

This geare *comm'th in pudding time*[16] rightlie.

He snatcht at the bag. No haste but good, (quoth
      shee),

Short shooting leeseth your game, ye may see,

Ye mist the cushin,[17] for all your haste to it.

And I may *set you beside the cushin* yit,

And *make you wipe your nose upon your sleeve,*

For ought you shall winne, without you aske me leeve.

Have yee not heard tell, *all covet, all leese?*

A sir, I see, *ye may see no greene cheese,*

But your teeth must water. A good cocknay coke:

Though he love not *to buy the pig in the poke,*

Yet snatch ye at the poke that the pig is in,

Not for the poke, but for the pig good cheape to win.

Like one halfe lost, till greedie grasping gat it

---

[16] *In pudding time.*

Formerly, when pudding was the first dish that was served, to
come in pudding time signified to be in time for dinner, or more
generally, to arrive in the nick of time.

      Our landlord did that shift prevent, ·
      Who came in pudding time and tooke his rent.
                      TAYLOR'S *Works*, 1630.

[17] *Ye mist the cushin.*

An idiomatic expression, meaning to fail in an undertaking;
takes its origin from the practice of archery.

Trulie, Euphues, you have mist the cushion, for I was neither
angrie with your long absence, neither am I well pleased at your
presence.—LYLY'S *Euphues.*

Ye would be over the stile ere ye come at it.[18]

But abide friend, your mother bid, till ye were borne,

Snatching winth it not, if ye snatch till to morne.

Men say, (said he), *long standing and small offring*

Maketh poore Parsons.   And in such signes and
      proffring

Many pretie tales and merrie toyes had they,

Before this bag came from her away.

Kindly he kist her with words not tart nor tough.

But *the cat knowth whose lips she lickth well enough.*[19]

Anone, the bag she delivered him, and sayd,

He should beare it, for that it now heavie wayd.

With good will, wife, for it is, (sayd he to her),

A proud horse that will not beare his owne provander.[20]

---

[18] *Ye would be over the stile*, &c.

Dulipo. I would fayne have you conclude.

Erostrato. You would fayne leape over the stile before you come
at the hedge.—GEORGE GASCOIGNE'S *Supposes*, 1575.

[19] *The cat knowth whose lips she lickth well enough.*

        Li vilains reproche du chat
        Qu'il set bien qui barbes il leche.
        Des trois Dames qui trouvèrent un anel, circa 1300.

[20] *A proud horse that will not bear his own provander.*

Nicholas. Indeed, I am patient, I must needes say, for patience
in adversitie brings a man to the Three Cranes in the Ventree.

Coomes. Do yee heere ? set downe your torche : drawe, fight, I
am for yee.

And oft before seemd she never so wise,

Yet was she now suddenly waxen *as nise,*

As it had been *a halfporth of silver spoones ;*

Thus clowdie mornings turne to cleere after noones.

But so nie noone it was, that by and by,

They rose and went to dinner lovingly.

CHAPTER X.

HIS dinner thought he long, and straight
after that,

  To his accustomed customers he gat.

With whom in what time he spent one grote before,

In lesse time he spent now ten grotes or more.

And in small time he brought the world so about,

That he brought the bottome of the bagge cleane out.

His gadding thus againe made her ill content :

But she not so much as dreamde that all was spent.

Howbeit suddenly she minded on a day,

Nicholas. And I am for yee too, though it be from the midnight
to the next morne.

Coomes. Where be your tooles ?

Nicholas. Within a mile of an oke, sir, hee's a proud horse that
will not carry his own provander, I warrant yee.—*Two Angry
Women of Abingdon,* 1599.

To pick the chest locke, wherein this bagge lay:
Determining this, if it lay whole still,
So shall it lye : no myte she minish will.
And if the bag began to shrinke, she thought best,
To take for her part some part of the rest.
But streight as she had forthwith opened the locke,
And look't in the bagge, what it was a clocke,
Then was it proved true, as this proverbe goth,
He that commeth last to the pot, is soonest wroth.
By her comming last, and too late to the pot,
Whereby she was potted thus like a sot,
To see the pot both skimd for running over,
And also all the licour runne at rover :
At her good husbands and her next meeting,
The divels good grace might have given a greeting,
Either for honour or honestie as good
As she gave him.   She was, (as they say), horne
        wood.
She netled him, and he ratled her so,
That at end of that fray, asunder they go,
And never after came together againe :
He turnd her out at doores to grase on the plaine ;
And himselfe went after.   For within fortnight,
All that was left, was launched out quight.
And thus had he *brought haddock to paddock*,
Till they both were not worth a haddock.

It hath been said, *neede maketh the old wife trot.*[1]
Other folke said it, but she did it, God wot;
First from frend to frend, and then from dur to dur,
A begging of some that had begged of hur.
But as men say, *miserie may be mother,*
Where one begger is driven to beg of another.
And thus wore and wasted this most wofull wretch,
Till death from this life, did her wretchedly fetch.
Her late husband, and now widowér, here and there
Wandring about, few know, and fewer care, where.
Cast out as an abject, he leadeth his life,
Till famine by like, set him after his wife.

Now let us note here. First of the first twaine,
Where they wedded, together to remaine,
Hoping joyfull presence should weare out all woe:
Yet povertie brought that joy to faile so.
But notably note these last twaine, where as he

---

[1] *Neede maketh the old wife trot.*

Thus travelling, a toiling trade I drive,
By reason of my age—neer seventy five,
It is my earthly portion and my lot,
The proverb says—" Need makes the old wife trot."
    A Merry Bill of an uncertaine Journey, by TAYLOR,
                the Water Poet.
        Besoin fait vieille trotter.
            Roman de Trubert, circa 1300.

Tooke her onely, for that he rich would be :
And she him onely in hope of good hap,
In her doting daies to be daunst on the lap.
In condition they differd so many waies,
That lightly he laid her up for holie daies.
Her good he laid up so, lest theeves might spie it,
That neither she could, nor he can come by it.
Thus failed all foure, of all things lesse and more,
Which they all, or any of all, maried fore.

CHAPTER XI.

ORSOOTH, (said my friend), this matter maketh bost
Of diminution,   For here is *a mill post,*
Thwitten to a pudding prick so neerely,
That I confesse me discouraged cleerely.
In both my weddings, in all things, except one :
This sparke of hope have I, to proceed upon.
Though these and some other, speed ill, as ye tell,
Yet other have lived and loved full well.
If I should deny that, (quoth I), I should rave :
For of both these sorts, I grant, that my self have

Seene of the tone sort, and heard of the tother,

That liked and lived right well, each with other.

But whether fortune will you, that man declare,

That shall choose in this choice, your comfort or care.

Since, before ye have chosen, we cannot know,

I thought to lay the worst, as ye the best show,

That ye might, being yet at libertie,

With all your joy, joyne all your jeopardie.

And now in this heard, in these cases on each part,

I say no more, but *lay your hand on your hart.*

I hartily thanke you (quoth he), I am sped

Of mine errand. *This hitteth the naile on the hed.*[2]

Who that leaveth suretie and leaveth unto chaunce,

When fooles pipe, by authoritie *he may daunce.*

And sure am I of those twaine, if I none choose,

Although I nought winne, yet shall I nought loose.

And to win a woman here, and lose a man,

In all this great winning what gain will I than?

---

[2] *Hitteth the naile on the hed.*

In an old anonymous play "my lord Cardinals players" are introduced, and in answer to the question as to what pieces compose their repertory, they reply :—

> Divers, my lord, The Cradle of Security,
> Hit nail o' th' head, Impatient Poverty,
> The Play of Four P's, Dives and Lazarus,
> Lusty Juventus, and the Marriage of Wit and Wisdom.
>   SIR THOMAS MORE.

But marke how follie hath me away caried :
How like a weathercock I have here varied.
First these two women to loose I was loth,
That if I might, I would have wedded them both.
Then thought I since, to have wedded one of them :
And now know I cleere, I will wed none of them.
They both shall have this one answere by letter ;
As good never a whit, as new the better.

Now let me aske, (quoth I), and your selfe answere,
The short question that I asked while ere,
A foule old rich widow, whether wed would ye,
Or a yong faire maide, being poore as ye be.
In neither barrel better herring,[3] (quoth he);
I like thus riches as ill as povertie.
Who that hath either of these pigges in me,
He hath *a pigge of the worse panier* sure.

---

[3] *In neither barrel better herring.*

An elliptical way of saying that no one barrel contains herrings
better than another. An early instance of its use occurs in a
work of Bishop Bale,—

Lyke Lord, lyke chaplayne, neyther barrel better herynge.
                                        Kynge John.

Again in BURTON'S *Anatomy of Melancholy*, 1621 :—Begin
where you will, you shall find them all alike, never a barrell the
better herring.

I was wedded unto my will.   Howbeit,

I will be divorst and wed to my wit.

Whereby with these examples past, I may see,

Fond wedding, for love, as good onely to flee.

Onely for love, or onely for good,

Or onely for both I wed not, by my hood.

Thus no one thing onely, though one thing chieflie

Shall woo me to wed now : for now I espie,

Although the chiefe one thing in wedding be love,

Yet must moe things joyne, as all in one may move,

Such kinde of living, for such kinde of life,

As lacking the same, *no lack to lack a wife.*

Here is enough, I am satisfied, (sayd he).

Since enough is enough, (sayd I), here may we

With that one word take end good, as may be geast :

For folke say, *enough is as good as a feast.*[4]

---

[4] *Enough is as good as a feast.*

It is an olde proverb He is well at ese y^t hath enough and can say ho.   He hath enough, holy doctours say, to whom his temporall godes be they never soo fewe suffisen to him and to his, to fynde them that them nedyth.—*Dives and Pauper,* 1493.

> And of enough enough, and nowe no more,
> Bycause my braynes no better can devise :
> When thinges be badde, a small summe maketh store
> So of suche verse a fewe may soone suffice ;
> Yet still to this my weary penne replyes.
> That I sayde last, and though like it least,
> It is enough and as good as a feast.
>
> GASCOIGNE'S *Memories,* 1575.

PRINTED BY WHITTINGHAM AND WILKINS,
TOOKS COURT, CHANCERY LANE.

A SELECTED LIST

OF

STANDARD PUBLICATIONS & REMAINDERS

Offered for Sale at remarkably low prices by

JOHN GRANT, BOOKSELLER,

25 & 34 George IV. Bridge,

EDINBURGH.

Moir's (D. M.) Works.

Poetical Works, with Portrait and Memoir, edited by Thomas Aird, 2 vols, fcap 8vo, cloth (pub 14s), 5s. Blackwood & Sons.

"These are volumes to be placed on the favourite shelf, in the familiar nook that holds the books we love, which we take up with pleasure and lay down with regret."—*Edinburgh Courant.*
"'Delta' has produced many pieces which will possess a permanent place in the poetry of Scotland."—Professor WILSON.

Lectures on the Poetical Literature of the Past Half-Century, fcap 8vo, cloth (pub 5s), 2s. Blackwood & Sons.

"A delightful volume ; exquisite in its taste, and generous in its criticisms." —HUGH MILLER.

Domestic Verses, fcap 8vo, cloth (pub 5s), 9d. Blackwood & Sons.

"This little work will be felt as a rich boon and treat to the feeling heart."— *Scotsman.*

Sent Carriage Free to any part of the United Kingdom on receipt of Postal Order for the amount.

JOHN GRANT, 25 & 34 George IV. Bridge, Edinburgh.

Beattie (James)—Poetical Works of, with Life, portrait and illustrations, crown 8vo, cloth extra, gilt edges (pub 2s 6d), 9d.
A neatly got up edition ; very suitable as a gift.

The New Library Edition of
The Works of Robert Burns, large paper copy, edited by W. Scott Douglas, with Explanatory Notes, Various Readings, and Glossary, illustrated with portraits, vignettes, and frontispieces, with India proof plates, by Sam Bough, R.S.A., and W. E. Lockhart, R.S.A., all newly engraved on steel, woodcuts, facsimiles, maps, and music, 6 vols, royal 8vo, cloth extra (pub £8 8s), £2 15s, W. Paterson, 1880.

*Lyndsay (Sir David, of the Mount)—*A Facsimile of the ancient Heraldic Manuscript emblazoned by the celebrated Sir David Lyndsay of the Mount, Lyon King at Arms in the reign of James the Fifth, edited by the late David Laing, LL.D., from the Original MS. in the possession of the Faculty of Advocates, folio, cloth, gilt top, uncut edges (pub £10 10s), £3 10s.
Impression limited to 250 copies.

Also Uniform.
Scottish Arms, being a Collection of Armorial Bearings, A.D. 1370-1678, Reproduced in Facsimile from Contemporary Manuscripts, with Heraldic and Genealogical Notes, by R. R. Stodart, of the Lyon Office, 2 vols, folio, cloth extra, gilt tops (pub £12 12s), £4 10s.
Impression limited to 300 copies.
Several of the manuscripts from which these Arms are taken have hitherto been unknown to heraldic antiquaries in this country. The Arms of upwards of 600 families are given, all of which are described in upwards of 400 pages of letterpress by Mr Stodart.
The book is uniform with Lyndsay's Heraldic Manuscript, and care was taken not to reproduce any Arms which are in that volume, unless there are variations, or from older manuscripts.

*Wilson (Professor)—The Comedy of the Noctes Ambros-*ianæ, by John Skelton, Advocate, with portraits of Wilson and Hogg, crown 8vo, cloth (pub 7s 6d), 3s, Blackwood & Sons.
"Mr Skelton has erected what is perhaps the most durable monument to Wilson's fame that we possess. In it we find the immortal trio at their best throughout. From beginning to end their meetings are inspired and sanctified by Bacchus and Apollo."—*Academy.*

Younger (John, shoemaker, St Boswells, Author of " River Angling for Salmon and Trout," " Corn Law Rhymes, &c.)—Autobiography, with portrait, crown 8vo (457 pages), cloth (pub 7s 6d), 2s 6d.
"'The shoemaker of St Boswells,' as he was designated in all parts of Scotland, was an excellent prose writer, a respectable poet, a marvellously gifted man in conversation. His life will be read with great interest ; the simple heart-stirring narrative of the life-struggle of a highly-gifted, humble, and honest mechanic,—a life of care, but also a life of virtue."—*London Review.*

Sent Carriage Free to any part of the United Kingdom on receipt of Postal Order for the amount.
JOHN GRANT, 25 & 34 George IV. Bridge, Edinburgh.

Historians of Scotland, complete set in 10 vols for £3 3s.

This Grand National Series of the Early Chronicles of Scotland, edited by the most eminent Scottish Antiquarian Scholars of the present day, is now completed, and as sets are becoming few in number, early application is necessary in order to secure them at the reduced price.

The Series comprises :—

Scoticronicon of John de Fordun, from the Contemporary MS. (if not the author's autograph) at the end of the Fourteenth Century, preserved in the Library of Wolfenbüttel, in the Duchy of Brunswick, collated with other known MSS. of the original chronicle, edited by W. F. Skene, LL.D., Historiographer Royal, 2 vols (pub 30s), not sold separately.

The Metrical Chronicle of Andrew Wyntoun, Prior of St Serf's Inch at Lochleven, who died about 1426, the work now printed entire for the first time, from the Royal MS. in the British Museum, collated with other MSS., edited by the late D. Laing, LL.D., 3 vols (pub 50s), vols 1 and 2 not sold separately. Vol 3 sold separately (pub 21s), 10s 6d.

Lives of Saint Ninian and St Kentigern, compiled in the 12th century, and edited from the best MSS. by the late A. P. Forbes, D.C.L., Bishop of Brechin (pub 15s), not sold separately.

Life of Saint Columba, founder of Hy, written by Adamnan, ninth Abbot of that Monastery, edited by Wm. Reeves, D.D., M.R.I.A., translated by the late A. P. Forbes, D.C.L., Bishop of Brechin, with Notes arranged by W. F. Skene, LL.D. (pub 15s), not sold separately.

The Book of Pluscarden, being unpublished Continuation of Fordun's Chronicle by M. Buchanan, Treasurer to the Dauphiness of France, edited and translated by Skene, 2 vols (pub 30s). Vol 2 separately (pub 12s 6d), 8s 6d.

A Critical Essay on the Ancient Inhabitants of Scotland, by Thomas Innes of the Sorbonne, with Memoir of the Author by George Grubb, LL.D., and Appendix of Original Documents by Wm. F. Skene, LL.D., illustrated with charts, out of print (pub 21s), 10s 6d.

In connection with the Society of Antiquaries of Scotland, a uniform series of the Historians of Scotland, accompanied by English translations, and illustrated by notes, critical and explanatory, was commenced some years since and has recently been finished.

So much has recently been done for the history of Scotland, that the necessity for a more critical edition of the earlier historians has become very apparent. The history of Scotland, prior to the 15th century, must always be based to a great extent upon the work of Fordun ; but his original text has been made the basis of continuations, and has been largely altered and interpolated by his continuators, whose statements are usually quoted as if they belonged to the original work of Fordun. An edition discriminating between the original text of Fordun and the additions and alterations of his continuators, and at the same time tracing out the sources of Fordun's narrative, would obviously be of great importance to the right understanding of Scottish history.

The complete set forms ten handsome volumes, demy 8vo, illustrated with facsimiles.

Sent Carriage Free to any part of the United Kingdom on receipt of Postal Order for the amount.

JOHN GRANT, 25 & 34 George IV. Bridge, Edinburgh.

Leighton's (Alexander) Mysterious Legends of Edinburgh,
illustrated, crown 8vo, cloth (pub 5s), 2s 6d.

CONTENTS:—Lord Kames' Puzzle, Mrs Corbet's Amputated Toe, The Brownie
of the West Bow, The Ancient Bureau, A Legend of Halkerstone's Wynd, Deacon
Macgillvray's Disappearance, Lord Braxfield's Case of the Red Night-cap, The
Strange Story of Sarah Gowanlock, and John Cameron's Life Policy.

*Steven's (Dr William) History of the High School of
Edinburgh,* from the beginning of the Sixteenth Century, based
upon Researches of the Town Council Records and other Authentic
Documents, illustrated with view, also facsimile of a School
Exercise by Sir Walter Scott when a pupil in 1783, crown 8vo,
cloth, a handsome volume (pub 7s 6d), 2s.

Appended is a list of the distinguished pupils who have been educated in this
Institution, which has been patronised by Royalty from the days of James VI.

*Exquisitely beautiful Works by Sir J. Noel Paton at a remarkably
low price.*

Paton's (Noel) Compositions from Shakespeare's Tempest,
a Series of Fifteen Large Outline Engravings illustrating the
Great Drama of our National Poet, with descriptive letterpress,
oblong folio, cloth (pub 21s), 3s. Chapman & Hall, 1845.

Uniform with the above.

*Paton's (Noel) Compositions from Shelley's Prometheus
Unbound,* a Series of Twelve Large Outline Engravings, oblong
folio, cloth (pub 21s), 3s. Chapman & Hall, 1846.

Pollok's (Robert) The Course of Time, a Poem, beautifully printed edition, with portrait and numerous illustrations,
12mo, cloth, 6d. Blackwood & Sons.

"'The Course of Time' is a very extraordinary poem, vast in its conception,
vast in its plan, vast in its materials, and vast, if very far from perfect, in its
achievement."—D. M. MOIR.

The Authorised Library Edition.

*Trial of the Directors of the City of Glasgow Bank, before
the Petition for Bail,* reported by Charles Tennant Couper,
Advocate, the Speeches and Opinions, revised by the Council and
Judges, and the Charge by the Lord Justice Clerk, illustrated
with lithographic facsimiles of the famous false Balance-sheets,
one large volume, royal 8vo, cloth (pub 15s), 3s 6d. Edinburgh.

History of the Queen's Edinburgh Rifle Volunteer Brigade,
with an Account of the City of Edinburgh and Midlothian Rifle
Association, the Scottish Twenty Club, &c., by Wm. Stephen,
crown 8vo, cloth (pub 5s), 2s 6d. Blackwood & Sons.

"This opportune volume has far more interest for readers generally than might
have been expected, while to members of the Edinburgh Volunteer Brigade it
cannot fail to be very interesting indeed."—*St James's Gazette.*

*Edinburgh University—Account of the Tercentenary Fes-
tival of the University,* including the Speeches and Addresses on
the Occasion, edited by R. Sydney Marsden, crown 8vo, cloth
(pub 3s), 1s 6d. Blackwood & Sons.

Grampian Club Publications, of valuable MSS.
and Works of Original Research in Scottish
History, Privately printed for the Members :—

The Diocesan Registers of Glasgow—Liber Protocollorum
M. Cuthberti Simonis, notarii et scribæ capituli Glasguensis, A.D.
1499-1513; also, *Rental Book of the Diocese of Glasgow*, A.D.
1509-1570, edited by Joseph Bain and the Rev. Dr Charles
Rogers, with facsimiles, 2 vols, 8vo, cl, 1875 (pub £2 2s), 10s 6d.

*Rental Book of the Cistercian Abbey of Coupar-Angus,
with the Breviary of the Register,* edited by the Rev. Dr Charles
Rogers, with facsimiles of MSS., 2 vols, 8vo, cloth, 1879-80 (pub
£2 12s 6d), 10s 6d.

———— The same, vol II., comprising the *Register of
Tacks of the Abbey of Cupar, Rental of St Marie's Monastery,* and
Appendix, 8vo, cloth (pub £1 1s), 3s 6d.

*Estimate of the Scottish Nobility during the Minority of
James VI.,* edited, with an Introduction, from the original MS.
in the Public Record Office, by Dr Charles Rogers, 8vo, cloth
(pub 10s 6d), 2s.

The reprint of a manuscript discovered in the Public Record Office. The
details are extremely curious.

Genealogical Memoirs of the Families of Colt and Coutts,
by Dr Charles Rogers, 8vo, cloth (pub 10s 6d), 2s 6d.

An old Scottish family, including the eminent bankers of that name, the
Baroness Burdett-Coutts, &c.

*Rogers' (Dr Charles) Memorials of the Earl of Stirling
and of the House of Alexander,* portraits, 2 vols, 8vo, cloth (pub
£3 3s), 10s 6d, Edinburgh, 1877.

This work embraces not only a history of Sir William Alexander, first Earl of
Stirling, but also a genealogical account of the family of Alexander in all its
branches; many interesting historical details connected with Scottish State affairs
in the seventeenth century; also with the colonisation of America.

---

*Sent Carriage Free to any part of the United Kingdom on
receipt of Postal Order for the amount.*

JOHN GRANT, 25 & 34 George IV. Bridge, Edinburgh.

Scott's (*Dr Hew*) *Fasti Ecclesiæ Scoticanæ*, Historical and
Biographical Notices of all the Ministers of the Church of Scotland from the Reformation, A.D. 1560, to the Present Time, 6
large vols, demy 4to, cloth, uncut (pub £9), £4 15s, Edinburgh, W. Paterson.

David Laing, the eminent antiquarian, considered this work a valuable and
necessary addition to the Bannatyne, Maitland, or Abbotsford Club Publications.
The work is divided into Synods, and where priced the volumes can be had
separately.

Vol 1.—Embraces Synods of Lothian and Tweeddale.   Not
sold separately.
Vol 2.—Synods of Merse and Teviotdale, Dumfries and Gal-
loway (pub 30s), 15s.
Vol 3.—Synods of Glasgow and Ayr (pub 30s), 15s.
Vol 4.—Synods of Fife, Perth, and Stirling (pub 30s), 15s.
Vol 5.—Synods of Argyll, Glenelg, Moray, Ross, Sutherland,
Caithness, Orkney, and Shetland, not sold separately.
Vol 6.—Synods of Aberdeen, and Angus and Mearns (pub
30s), 15s.

Historical Sketches of the Highland Clans of Scotland,
containing a concise account of the origin, &c., of the Scottish
Clans, with twenty-two illustrative coloured plates of the Tartan
worn by each, post 8vo, cloth, 2s 6d.

"The object of this treatise is to give a concise account of the origin, seat,
and characteristics of the Scottish Clans, together with a representation of the
distinguishing tartan worn by each."—*Preface.*

Historical Geography of the Clans of Scotland, by T. B.
Johnston, F.R.G.S., F.R.S.E., and F.S.A.S., Geographer to
the Queen, and Colonel James A. Robertson, F.S.A.S., demy 4to,
cloth, with a map of Scotland divided into Clans (large folding
map, coloured) (pub 7s 6d), Keith Johnston, 3s. 6d.

"The map bears evidence of careful preparation, and the editor acknowledges
the assistance of Dr William Skene, who is known for eminent services to Highland archæology."—*Athenæum.*

Keltie's (*John S.*) *History of the Scottish Highlands,*
Highland Clans, and Highland Regiments, with an account of the
Gaelic Language, Literature, Music, &c., illustrated with portraits,
views, maps, &c., engraved on steel, clan tartans, numerous
woodcuts, including armorial bearings, 2 vols, imperial 8vo, half
morocco (pub £3 10s), £1 17s 6d.

*Sent Carriage Free to any part of the United Kingdom on
receipt of Postal Order for the amount.*

JOHN GRANT, 25 & 34 George IV. Bridge, Edinburgh.

Burt's (*Capt.*) *Letters from the North of Scotland* (*1754*), with an Introduction by R. Jamieson, F.S.A. ; and the History of Donald the Hammerer, from an authentic account of the Family of Invernahyle, a MS. communication by Sir Walter Scott, with facsimiles of all the original engravings, 2 vols, 8vo, cloth (pub 21s), 8s 6d. W. Paterson.

"Captain Burt was one of the first Englishmen who caught a glimpse of the spots which now allure tourists from every part of the civilised world, at a time when London had as little to do with the Grampians as with the Andes. The author was evidently a man of a quick, an observant, and a cultivated mind."— LORD MACAULAY.
"An extremely interesting and curious work."—LOWNDES.

Chambers's (*William, of Glenormiston*) *History of Peebles-shire*, its Local Antiquities, Geology, Natural History, &c., with one hundred engravings, vignettes, and coloured map from Ordnance Survey, royal 8vo, cloth (pub £1 11s 6d), 9s. W. Paterson.

"To the early history and antiquities of this district, and to old names and old families connected with the place, Mr Chambers lends a charm which is not often met with in such subjects. He discerns the usefulness of social as well as political history, and is pleasantly aware that the story of manners and morals and customs is as well worth telling as the story of man," &c.—*Athenæum.*

Douglas' (*Gavin, Bishop of Dunkeld, 1475-1522*) *Poetical Works*, edited, with Memoir, Notes, and full Glossary, by John Small, M.A., F.S.A. Scot., illustrated with specimens of manu-script, title-page, and woodcuts of the early editions in facsimile, 4 vols, beautifully printed on thick paper, post 8vo, cloth (pub £3 3s), £1 2s 6d. W. Paterson.

"The latter part of the fifteenth and beginning of the sixteenth century, a period almost barren in the annals of English poetry, was marked by a remark-able series of distinguished poets in Scotland. During this period flourished Dunbar, Henryson, Mercier, Harry the Minstrel, Gavin Douglas, Bellenden, Kennedy, and Lyndesay. Of these, although the palm of excellence must beyond all doubt be awarded to Dunbar,—next to Burns probably the greatest poet of his country,—the voice of contemporaries, as well as of the age that immediately followed, pronounced in favour of him who,
'In barbarous age,
Gave rude Scotland Virgil's page,'—
Gavin Douglas. We may confidently predict that this will long remain the standard edition of Gavin Douglas ; and we shall be glad to see the works of other of the old Scottish poets edited with equal sympathy and success."—*Athenæum.*

Lyndsay's (*Sir David, of the Mount, 1490-1568*) *Poetical Works*, best edition, edited, with Life, Notes, and Glossary, by David Laing, 3 vols, crown 8vo, cloth (pub 63s), 18s 6d. W. Paterson.

"When it is said that the revision, including Preface, Memoir, and Notes, has been executed by Dr David Laing, it is said that all has been done that is possible by thorough scholarship, good judgment, and conscientiousness."— *Scotsman.*

Sent Carriage Free to any part of the United Kingdom on receipt of Postal Order for the amount.

JOHN GRANT, 25 & 34 George IV. Bridge, Edinburgh.

Crieff: Its Traditions and Characters, with Anecdotes of Strathearn, Reminiscences of Obsolete Customs, Traditions, and Superstitions, Humorous Anecdotes of Schoolmasters, Ministers, and other Public Men, crown 8vo, 1s.

"A book which will have considerable value in the eyes of all collectors of Scottish literature. A gathering up of stories about well-known inhabitants, memorable local occurrences, and descriptions of manners and customs."— *Scotsman.*

Dunfermline—Henderson's Annals of Dunfermline and Vicinity, from the earliest Authentic Period to the Present Time, A.D. 1069-1878, interspersed with Explanatory Notes, Memorabilia, and numerous illustrative engravings, large vol, 4to, half morocco, gilt top (pub 21s), 6s 6d.

The genial Author of " Noctes Ambrosianæ."

Christopher North—A Memoir of Professor John Wilson, compiled from Family Papers and other sources, by his daughter, Mrs Gordon, new edition, with portrait and illustrations, crown 8vo, cloth (pub 6s), 2s 6d.

" A writer of the most ardent and enthusiastic genius."—HENRY HALLAM.
" The whole literature of England does not contain a more brilliant series of articles than those with which Wilson has enriched the pages of *Blackwood's Magazine.*"—Sir ARCHIBALD ALISON.

The Cloud of Witnesses for the Royal Prerogatives of Jesus Christ; or, The Last Speeches and Testimonies of those who have Suffered for the Truth in Scotland since the year 1680, best edition, by the Rev. J. H. Thompson, numerous illustrations, handsome volume, 8vo, cloth gilt (pub 7s 6d), 4s 6d.

"The interest in this remarkable book can never die, and to many we doubt not this new and handsome edition will be welcome."—*Aberdeen Herald.*
"Altogether it is like a resurrection, and the vision of Old Mortality, as it passes over the scenes of his humble but solemn and sternly significant labours, seems transfigured in the bright and embellished pages of the modern reprint."— *Daily Review.*

M'Kerlie's (P. H., F.S.A. Scot.) History of the Lands and their Owners in Galloway, illustrated by woodcuts of Notable Places and Objects, with a Historical Sketch of the District, 5 handsome vols, crown 8vo, roxburghe style (pub £3 15s), 26s 6d. W. Paterson.

Wilson's (Dr Daniel) Memorials of Edinburgh in the Olden Time, with numerous fine engravings and woodcuts, 2 vols, 4to, cloth (pub £2 2s), 16s 6d.

Hamilton's (Lady, the Mistress of Lord Nelson) Attitudes, illustrating in 25 full-page plates the great Heroes and Heroines of Antiquity in their proper Costume, forming a useful study for drawing from correct and chaste models of Grecian and Roman Sculpture, 4to, cloth (pub £1 1s), 3s 6d.

Sent Carriage Free to any part of the United Kingdom on receipt of Postal Order for the amount.

JOHN GRANT, 25 & 34 George IV. Bridge, Edinburgh.

Hay's (D. R.) Science of Beauty, as Developed in Nature and Applied in Art, 23 full-page illustrations, royal 8vo, cloth (pub 10s 6d), 2s 6d.

Art and Letters, an Illustrated Magazine of Fine Art and Fiction, edited by J. Comyns Carr, complete year 1882-83, handsome volume, folio, neatly bound in bevelled cloth, gilt top, edges uncut, and Parts 1 and 2 of the succeeding year, when the publication ceased, illustrated with many hundred engravings in the highest style of art, including many of the choicest illustrations of "L'Art," published by arrangement with the French proprietors (pub £1 1s), 8s 6d.

> The artistic excellence of this truly handsome volume commends itself to all lovers of what is beautiful in nature and art. The illustrations, which are numerous and varied, embrace—Specimens of Sculpture Old and New, Facsimile Drawings of the Old Masters, Examples of Art Furniture, with objects exhibited in the great European Collections, Animals in Art illustrated by Examples in Painting and Sculpture, Art on the Stage, Products of the Keramic Art Ancient and Modern, the various forms of Art Industry, &c. &c., accompanied by interesting articles by men thoroughly acquainted with the various subjects introduced.

Stewart's (Dugald) Collected Works, best edition, edited by Sir William Hamilton, with numerous Notes and Emendations, 11 handsome vols, 8vo, cloth (pub £6 12s), the few remaining sets for £2 10s. T. & T. Clark.

Sold Separately,

Elements of the Philosophy of the Human Mind, 3 vols, 8vo, cloth (pub £1 16s), 12s.

Philosophy of the Active Powers, 2 vols, 8vo, cloth (pub £1 4s), 10s.

Principles of Political Economy, 2 vols, 8vo, cloth (pub £1 4s), 10s.

Biographical Memoirs of Adam Smith, Principal Robertson, and Thomas Reid, 8vo, cloth (pub 12s), 4s 6d.

Supplementary Volume, with General Index, 8vo, cloth (pub 12s), 5s.

> " As the names of Thomas Reid, of Dugald Stewart, and of Sir William Hamilton will be associated hereafter in the history of Philosophy in Scotland, as closely as those of Xenophanes, Parmenides, and Zeno in the School of Elea, it is a singular fortune that Sir William Hamilton should be the collector and editor of the works of his predecessors. . . . The chair which he filled for many years, not otherwise undistinguished, he rendered illustrious."— *Athenæum.*

Sent Carriage Free to any part of the United Kingdom on receipt of Postal Order for the amount.

JOHN GRANT, 25 & 34 George IV. Bridge, Edinburgh.

Campbell (Colin, Lord Clyde)—Life of, illustrated by Extracts from his Diary and Correspondence, by Lieut.-Gen. Shadwell, C.B., with portrait, maps, and Plans, 2 vols, 8vo, cloth (pub 36s), 10s 6d, Blackwood & Sons.

"In all the annals of 'Self-Help,' there is not to be found a life more truly worthy of study than that of the gallant old soldier. The simple, self-denying, friend-helping, brave, patriotic soldier stands proclaimed in every line of General Shadwell's admirable memoir."—*Blackwood's Magazine.*

Crime—Pike's (Luke Owen) History of Crime in England, illustrating the Changes of the Laws in the Progress of Civilisation from the Roman Invasion to the Present Time, Index, 2 very thick vols, 8vo, cloth (pub 36s) 10s, Smith, Elder, & Co.

Creasy (Sir Edward S.)—History of England, from the Earliest Times to the End of the Middle Ages, 2 vols (520 pp each), 8vo, cloth (pub 25s), 6s, Smith, Elder, & Co.

Garibaldi—The Red Shirt, Episodes of the Italian War, by Alberto Mario, crown 8vo, cloth (pub 6s), 1s, Smith, Elder, & Co.

"These episodes read like chapters in the ' History of the Seven Champions; ' they give vivid pictures of the incidents of that wonderful achievement, the triumphal progress from Sicily to Naples ; and the incidental details of the difficulties, dangers, and small reverses which occurred during the progress, remove the event from the region of enchantment to the world of reality and human heroism."—*Athenæum.*

History of the War of Frederick I. against the Communes of Lombardy, by Giovanni B. Testa, translated from the Italian, and dedicated by the Author to the Right Hon. W. E. Gladstone, (466 pages), 8vo, cloth (pub 15s) 2s, Smith, Elder, & Co.

Martineau (Harriet)—The History of British Rule in India, foolscap 8vo (356 pages), cloth (pub 2s 6d), 1s, Smith, Elder, & Co.

A concise sketch, which will give the ordinary reader a general notion of what our Indian empire is, how we came by it, and what has gone forward in it since it first became connected with England. The book will be found to state the broad facts of Anglo-Indian history in a clear and enlightening manner ; and it cannot fail to give valuable information to those readers who have neither time nor inclination to study the larger works on the subject.

Mathews (Charles James, the Actor)—Life of, chiefly Autobiographical, with Selections from his Correspondence and Speeches, edited by Charles Dickens, portraits, 2 vols, 8vo, cloth (pub 25s), 5s, Macmillan, 1879.

"The book is a charming one from first to last, and Mr Dickens deserves a full measure of credit for the care and discrimination he has exercised in the business of editing."—*Globe.*
" Mr Dickens's interesting work, which should be read by all students of the stage."—*Saturday Review.*

Reumont (Alfred von)—Lorenzo de Medici, the Magnificent, translated from the German, by Robert Harrison, 2 vols, 8vo, cloth (pub 30s), 6s 6d, Smith, Elder, & Co.

Sent Carriage Free to any part of the United Kingdom on receipt of Postal Order for the amount.

JOHN GRANT, 25 & 34 George IV. Bridge, Edinburgh.

Oliphant (Laurence)—The Land of Gilead, with Excursions in the Lebanon, illustrations and maps, 8vo, cloth (pub 21s), 8s 6d, Blackwood & Sons.

"A most fascinating book."—*Observer.*

"A singularly agreeable narrative of a journey through regions more replete, perhaps, with varied and striking associations than any other in the world. The writing throughout is highly picturesque and effective."—*Athenæum.*

"A most fascinating volume of travel. . . . His remarks on manners, customs, and superstitions are singularly interesting."—*St James's Gazette.*

"The reader will find in this book a vast amount of most curious and valuable information on the strange races and religions scattered about the country."—*Saturday Review.*

"An admirable work, both as a record of travel and as a contribution to physical science."—*Vanity Fair.*

Patterson (R. H.)—The New Golden Age, and Influence of the Precious Metals upon the War, 2 vols, 8vo, cloth (pub 31s 6d), 6s, Blackwood & Sons.

CONTENTS.

VOL I.—THE PERIOD OF DISCOVERY AND ROMANCE OF THE NEW GOLDEN AGE, 1848-56.—The First Tidings—Scientific Fears, and General Enthusiasm—The Great Emigration—General Effects of the Gold Discoveries upon Commerce—Position of Great Britain, and First Effects on it of the Gold Discoveries—The Golden Age in California and Australia—Life at the Mines. A RETROSPECT.—History and Influence of the Precious Metals down to the Birth of Modern Europe—The Silver Age in America—Effects of the Silver Age upon Europe—Production of the Precious Metals during the Silver Age (1492-1810)—Effects of the Silver Age upon the Value of Money (1492-1800).

VOL II.—PERIOD OF RENEWED SCARCITY.—Renewed Scarcity of the Precious Metals, A.D. 1800-30—The Period of Scarcity. Part II.—Effects upon Great Britain—The Scarcity lessens—Beginnings of a New Gold Supply—General Distress before the Gold Discoveries. "CHEAP" AND "DEAR" MONEY—On the Effects of Changes in the Quantity and Value of Money. THE NEW GOLDEN AGE.—First Getting of the New Gold—First Diffusion of the New Gold—Industrial Enterprise in Europe—Vast Expansion of Trade with the East (A.D. 1855-75)—Total Amount of the New Gold and Silver—Its Influence upon the World at large—Close of the Golden Age, 1876-80—Total Production of Gold and Silver. PERIOD 1492-1848.—Production of Gold and Silver subsequent to 1848—Changes in the Value of Money subsequent to A.D. 1492. PERIOD A.D. 1848 and subsequently. PERIOD A.D. 1782-1865.—Illusive Character of the Board of Trade Returns since 1853—Growth of our National Wealth.

Richardson and Watts' Complete Practical Treatise on Acids, Alkalies, and Salts, their Manufacture and Application, by Thomas Richardson, Ph.D., F.R.S., &c., and Henry Watts, F.R.S., F.C.S., &c., illustrated with numerous wood engravings, 3 thick 8vo vols, cloth (pub £4 10s), 8s 6d, London.

Tunis, Past and Present, with a Narrative of the French Conquest of the Regency, by A. M. Broadley, Correspondent of the *Times* during the War in Tunis, with numerous illustrations and maps, 2 vols, post 8vo, cloth (pub 25s), 6s, Blackwood & Sons.

"Mr Broadley has had peculiar facilities in collecting materials for his volumes. Possessing a thorough knowledge of Arabic, he has for years acted as confidential adviser to the Bey. . . . The information which he is able to place before the reader is novel and amusing. . . . A standard work on Tunis has been long required. This deficiency has been admirably supplied by the author."—*Morning Post.*

Cervantes—History of the Ingenious Gentleman, Don Quixote of La Mancha, translated from the Spanish by P. A. Motteux, illustrated with a portrait and 36 etchings, by M. A. Laluze, illustrator of the library edition of Moliere's Works, 4 vols, large 8vo, cloth (sells £3 12s), £1 15s. W. Paterson.

Dyer (Thomas H., LL.D.)—Imitative Art, its Principles and Progress, with Preliminary Remarks on Beauty, Sublimity, and Taste, 8vo, cloth (pub 14s), 2s. Bell & Sons, 1882.

Junior Etching Club—Passages from Modern English Poets, Illustrated by the Junior Etching Club, 47 beautiful etchings by J. E. Millais, J. Whistler, J. Tenniel, Viscount Bury, J. Lawless, F. Smallfield, A. J. Lewis, C. Rossiter, and other artists, 4to, cloth extra, gilt edges (pub 15s), 4s.

Smith (J. Moyr)—Ancient Greek Female Costume, illustrated by 112 fine outline engravings and numerous smaller illustrations, with Explanatory Letterpress, and Descriptive Passages from the Works of Homer, Hesiod, Herodotus, Æschylus, Euripides, and other Greek Authors, printed in brown, crown 8vo, cloth elegant, red edges (pub 7s 6d), 3s. Sampson Low.

Strutt's Sylva Britanniæ et Scotiæ ; or, Portraits of Forest Trees Distinguished for their Antiquity, Magnitude, or Beauty, drawn from Nature, with 50 highly finished etchings, imp. folio, half morocco extra, gilt top, a handsome volume (pub £9 9s), £2 2s.

Walpole's (Horace) Anecdotes of Painting in England, with some Account of the Principal Artists, enlarged by Rev. James Dallaway ; and Vertue's Catalogue of Engravers who have been born or resided in England, last and best edition, revised with additional notes by Ralph N. Wornum, illustrated with eighty portraits of the principal artists, and woodcut portraits of the minor artists, 3 handsome vols, 8vo, cloth (pub 27s), 14s 6d. Bickers.

—— The same, 3 vols, half morocco, gilt top, by one of the best Edinburgh binders (pub 45s), £1 8s.

*Warren's (Samuel) Works—*Original and early editions as follows :—

Miscellanies, Critical, Imaginative, and Juridical, contributed to *Blackwood's Magazine,* original edition, 2 vols, post 8vo, cloth (pub 24s), 5s. Blackwood, 1855.

Now and Then ; Through a Glass Darkly, early edition, crown 8vo, cloth (pub 6s), 1s 6d. Blackwood, 1853.

Ten Thousand a Year,, early edition, with Notes, 3 vols, 12mo, boards, back paper title (pub 18s), 4s 6d. Blackwood, 1853.

Sent Carriage Free to any part of the United Kingdom on receipt of Postal Order for the amount.

JOHN GRANT, 25 & 34 George IV. Bridge, Edinburgh.

Wood (*Major Herbert, R.E.*)—*The Shores of Lake Aral*, with large folding maps (352 pages), 8vo, cloth (pub 14s), 2s 6d, Smith, Elder, & Co.

Arnold's (*Cecil*) *Great Sayings of Shakespeare*, a Comprehensive Index to Shakespearian Thought, being a Collection of Allusions, Reflections, Images, Familiar and Descriptive Passages, and Sentiments from the Poems and Plays of Shakespeare, Alphabetically Arranged and Classified under Appropriate Headings, one handsome volume of 422 pages, thick 8vo, cloth (pub 7s 6d), 3s. Bickers.

Arranged in a manner similar to Southgate's "Many Thoughts of Many Minds." This index differs from all other books in being much more comprehensive, while care has been taken to follow the most accurate text, and to cope, in the best manner possible, with the difficulties of correct classification.

Bacon (*Francis, Lord*)—*Works*, both English and Latin, with an Introductory Essay, Biographical and Critical, and copious Indices, steel portrait, 2 vols, royal 8vo, cloth (originally pub £2 2s,) 12s, 1879.

"All his works are, for expression as well as thought, the glory of our nation, and of all later ages."—SHEFFIELD, Duke of Buckinghamshire.

"Lord Bacon was more and more known, and his books more and more delighted in; so that those men who had more than ordinary knowledge in human affairs, esteemed him one of the most capable spirits of that age."

Burnet (*Bishop*)—*History of the Reformation of the Church of England*, with numerous Illustrative Notes and copious Index, 2 vols, royal 8vo, cloth (pub 20s), 10s, Reeves & Turner, 1880.

"Burnet, in his immortal History of the Reformation, has fixed the Protestant religion in this country as long as any religion remains among us. Burnet is, without doubt, the English Eusebius."—Dr APTHORPE.

Burnet's *History of his Own Time*, from the Restoration of Charles II. to the Treaty of the Peace of Utrecht, with Historical and Biographical Notes, and a copious Index, complete in 1 thick volume, imperial 8vo, portrait, cloth (pub £1 5s), 5s 6d.

"I am reading Burnet's Own Times. Did you ever read that garrulous pleasant history? full of scandal, which all true history is; no palliatives, but all the stark wickedness that actually gave the *momentum* to national actors; none of that cursed *Humeian* indifference, so cold, and unnatural, and inhuman," &c. —CHARLES LAMB.

Dante—*The Divina Commedia*, translated into English Verse by James Ford, A.M., medallion frontispiece, 430 pages, crown 8vo, cloth, bevelled boards (pub 12s), 2s 6d. Smith, Elder, & Co.

"Mr Ford has succeeded better than might have been expected; his rhymes are good, and his translation deserves praise for its accuracy and fidelity. We cannot refrain from acknowledging the many good qualities of Mr Ford's translation, and his labour of love will not have been in vain, if he is able to induce those who enjoy true poetry to study once more the masterpiece of that literature from whence the great founders of English poetry drew so much of their sweetness and power."—*Athenæum.*

Sent Carriage Free to any part of the United Kingdom on receipt of Postal Order for the amount.

JOHN GRANT, 25 & 34 George IV. Bridge, Edinburgh.

Dobson (W. T.)—The Classic Poets, their Lives and their Times, with the Epics Epitomised, 452 pages, crown 8vo, cloth (pub 9s), 2s 6d. Smith, Elder, & Co.

CONTENTS.—Homer's Iliad, The Lay of the Nibelungen, Cid Campeador, Dante's Divina Commedia, Ariosto's Orlando Furioso, Camoens' Lusiad, Tasso's Jerusalem Delivered, Spenser's Fairy Queen, Milton's Paradise Lost, Milton's Paradise Regained.

English Literature : A Study of the Prologue and Epilogue in English Literature, from Shakespeare to Dryden, by G. S. B., crown 8vo, cloth (pub 5s), 1s 6d. Kegan Paul, 1884.

Will no doubt prove useful to writers undertaking more ambitious researches into the wider domains of dramatic or social history.

Johnson (Doctor)—His Friends and his Critics, by George Birkbeck Hill, D.C.L., crown 8vo, cloth (pub 8s), 2s. Smith, Elder, & Co.

"The public now reaps the advantage of Dr Hill's researches in a most readable volume. Seldom has a pleasanter commentary been written on a literary masterpiece. . . . Throughout the author of this pleasant volume has spared no pains to enable the present generation to realise more completely the sphere in which Johnson talked and taught."—*Saturday Review.*

Jones' (Rev. Harry) East and West London, being Notes of Common Life and Pastoral Work in St James's, Westminster, and in St George's-in-the-East, crown 8vo, cloth (pub 6s), 2s. Smith, Elder, & Co.

"Mr Jones gives a graphic description of the trades and industries of East London, of the docks and their multifarious populations, of the bonded stores, of Jamrach and his wild animal repository, of Ratcliffe Highway with its homes and its snares for sailors, until the reader finds himself at home with all sorts and conditions of strange life and folk. . . . A better antidote to recent gloomy forebodings of our national decadence can hardly be found."—*Athenæum.*

Kaye (John William, F.R.S., author of " History of the War in Afghanistan ")—The Essays of an Optimist, crown 8vo, cloth extra (pub 6s), 1s 6d. Smith, Elder, & Co.

"The Essays are seven in number,—Holidays, Work, Success, Toleration, Rest, Growing Old, and the Wrong Side of the Stuff,—themes on which the author discourses with bright and healthy vigour, good sense, and good taste."—*Standard.*

" We most sincerely trust that this book may find its way into many an English household. It cannot fail to instil lessons of manliness."—*Westminster Review.*

Selkirk (J. B.)—Ethics and Æsthetics of Modern Poetry, crown 8vo, cloth gilt (pub 7s), 2s. Smith, Elder, & Co.

Sketches from Shady Places, being Sketches from the Criminal and Lower Classes, by Thor Fredur, crown 8vo, cloth (pub 6s), 1s. Smith, Elder, & Co.

" Descriptions of the criminal and semi-criminal (if such a word may be coined) classes, which are full of power, sometimes of a disagreeable kind."—*Athenæum.*

£ S. D.

By the Authoress of " The Land o' the Leal."

Nairne's (Baroness) Life and Songs, with a
Memoir, and Poems of Caroline Oliphant the Younger, edited
by Dr Charles Rogers, *portrait and other illustrations*, crown
8vo, cloth (pub 5s) Griffin   0   2   6
" This publication is a good service to the memory of an excellent and gifted
lady, and to all lovers of Scottish Song."—*Scotsman.*

Ossian's Poems, translated by Macpherson,
24mo, best red cloth, gilt (pub 2s 6d)   0   1   6
A dainty pocket edition.

Perthshire—Woods, Forests, and Estates of
Perthshire, with Sketches of the Principal Families of the
County, by Thomas Hunter, Editor of the *Perthshire Consti-
tutional and Journal, illustrated with 30 wood engravings*,
crown 8vo (564 pp.), cloth (pub 12s 6d) Perth   0   6   0
" Altogether a choice and most valuable addition to the County Histories of
Scotland."—*Glasgow Daily Mail.*

Duncan (John, Scotch Weaver and Botanist)
—Life of, with Sketches of his Friends and Notices of the
Times, by Wm. Jolly, F.R.S.E., H.M. Inspector of Schools,
etched portrait, crown 8vo, cloth (pub 9s) Kegan Paul   0   4   0
" We must refer the reader to the book itself for the many quaint traits of
character, and the minute personal descriptions, which, taken together, seem to
give a life-like presentation of this humble philosopher. . . . The many incidental notices which the work contains of the weaver caste, the workman's
esprit de corps, and his wanderings about the country, either in the performance
of his work or, when that was slack, taking a hand at the harvest, form an interesting chapter of social history. The completeness of the work is considerably
enhanced by detailed descriptions of the district he lived in, and of his numerous
friends and acquaintance."—*Athenæum.*

Scots (Ancient)—An Examination of the An-
cient History of Ireland and Iceland, in so far as it concerns
the Origin of the Scots; Ireland not the Hibernia of the
Ancients; Interpolations in Bede's Ecclesiastical History and
other Ancient Annals affecting the Early History of Scotland
and Ireland—the three Essays in one volume, crown 8vo, cloth
(pub 4s) Edinburgh, 1883   0   1   0
The first of the above treatises is mainly taken up with an investigation of the
early History of Ireland and Iceland, in order to ascertain which has the better
claim to be considered the original country of the Scots. In the second and
third an attempt is made to show that Iceland was the ancient Hibernia, and
the country from which the Scots came to Scotland; and further, contain a
review of the evidence furnished by the more genuine of the early British Annals
against the idea that Ireland was the ancient Scotia.

Magic and Astrology—Grant (James)—The
Mysteries of all Nations: Rise and Progress of Superstition,
Laws against and Trials of Witches, Ancient and Modern
Delusions, together with Strange Customs, Fables, and Tales
relating to Mythology, Miracles, Poets, and Superstition,
Demonology, Magic and Astrology, Trials by Ordeal, Superstition in the Nineteenth Century, &c., 1 thick vol, 8vo, cloth
(pub 12s 6d) 1880   0   2   6
An interesting work on the subject of Superstition, valuable alike to archæo-
logists and general readers. It is chiefly the result of antiquarian research and
actual observation during a period of nearly forty years.

A Story of the Shetland Isles.

Saxby (*Jessie M.*, author of " *Daala-Mist*," &c.)—*Rock-Bound*, a Story of the Shetland Isles, second edition, revised, crown 8vo, cloth (pub 2s), 6d. Edinburgh, 1877.

"The life I have tried to depict is the life I remember twenty years ago, when the islands were far behind the rest of Britain in all that goes to make up modern civilisation."—*Extract from Preface.*

Burn (*R. Scott*)—*The Practical Directory for the Improvement* of Landed Property, Rural and Suburban, and the Economic Cultivation of its Farms (the most valuable work on the subject), plates and woodcuts, 2 vols, 4to, cloth (pub £3 3s), 15s, Paterson.

Burnet's *Treatise on Painting, illustrated by 130 Etchings* from celebrated pictures of the Italian, Venetian, Flemish, Dutch, and English Schools, also woodcuts, thick 4to, half morocco, gilt top (pub £4 10s), £2 2s.

The Costumes of all Nations, Ancient and Modern, exhibiting the Dresses and Habits of all Classes, Male and Female, from the Earliest Historical Records to the Nineteenth Century, by Albert Kretschmer and Dr Rohrbach, 104 coloured plates displaying nearly 2000 full-length figures, complete in one handsome volume, 4to, half morocco (pub £4 4s), 45s, Sotheran.

Dryden's *Dramatic Works, Library Edition, with Notes* and Life by Sir Walter Scott, Bart., edited by George Saintsbury, portrait and plates, 8 vols, 8vo, cloth (pub £4 4s), £1 10s, Paterson.

Lessing's (*Dr J.*) *Ancient Oriental Carpet Patterns*, after Pictures and Originals of the 15th and 16th Centuries, 35 plates (size 20 × 14 in.), beautifully coloured after the originals, 1 vol, royal folio, in portfolio (pub £3 3s), 21s, Sotheran.

The most beautiful Work on the " Stately Homes of England."

Nash's *Mansions of England in the Olden Time, 104* Lithographic Views faithfully reproduced from the originals, with new and complete history of each Mansion, by Anderson, 4 vols in 2, imperial 4to, cloth extra, gilt edges (pub £6 6s), £2 10s, Sotheran.

Richardson's (*Samuel*) *Works, Library Edition, with* Biographical Criticism by Leslie Stephen, portrait, 12 vols, 8vo, cloth extra, impression strictly limited to 750 copies (pub £6 6s), £2 5s, London.

Sent Carriage Free to any part of the United Kingdom on receipt of Postal Order for the amount.

JOHN GRANT, 25 & 34 George IV. Bridge, Edinburgh.

COLUMBIA UNIVERSITY LIBRARIES

This book is due on the date indicated below, or at the expiration of a definite period after the date of borrowing, as provided by the library rules or by special arrangement with the Librarian in charge.

DATE BORROWED	DATE DUE	DATE BORROWED	DATE DUE
	NOV 9 1950		
	MAY 29 1951		

C28 (1149) 100M

CPSIA information can be obtained
at www.ICGtesting.com
Printed in the USA
LVHW041611070223
738891LV00004B/292